It's time for the 21st-century Church
to return to a 1st-century vision

GOD'S BLUEPRINT
for His Church

Andy Elmes

DESTINY IMAGE™ EUROPE srl
Via Maiella, 1
66020 San Giovanni Teatino (Ch) – Italy

"Changing the World, One Book at a Time."

This book and all other Evangelista Media™ and Destiny Image™ Europe books are available at Christian bookstores and distributors worldwide.

To order products, or for any other correspondence:

EVANGELISTA MEDIA™ srl
Via della Scafa 29/14
65013 Città Sant'Angelo (Pe) – Italy
Tel. +39 085 4716623 • Fax: +39 085 9090113
Email: info@evangelistamedia.com
Or reach us on the Internet: www.evangelistamedia.com

ISBN 13: 978-88-96727-96-6
ISBN 13 EBOOK: 978-88-96727-98-0

For Worldwide Distribution, Printed in the U.S.A.
1 2 3 4 5 6 / 15 14 13 12

DEDICATION

To my beautiful wife, Gina:

As God opens so many exciting new doors, I am so glad I get to walk through them hand in hand with you. You are the perfect wife for me and my best and dearest friend; I thank God for you, always. Together let's step into the next part of the adventure God has for us.

Love you,

Andy

ENDORSEMENTS

Although many Christian authors attempt to address the condition of the Church, few have managed to impart such poignant commentary and personal insight as Andy Elmes in *God's Blueprint for His Church*—a tour de force communicated with apostolic authority and prophetic clarity. By examining firsthand experiences within his own church, Andy provides perceptive recommendations with the discernment that only comes from experience.

Andy not only writes with the skill of an author, but with the palpable artistry of a "master builder." His work petitions other co-laborers at all levels of spiritual maturity to build wisely, according to the original blueprint. By emphasizing the potential and purpose of the Church, *God's Blueprint for His Church* awakens confidence that the gates of hell will not prevail.

The contents of this book will help shape a new generation of leaders, pastors, and ministers who are tired of a church system that caters to the lazy and spiritually indifferent. Andy Elmes inspires an ongoing dialogue that will engage all who are eager to enter into a radical new era—one in which the Church exists solely for the glory of God: "…to Him be glory in the church by Christ Jesus to all generations, forever and ever. Amen" (Eph. 3:21).

Dr. Leon van Rooyen, President
Global Ministries and Relief

God's Blueprint for His Church by my dear friend, Andy Elmes, is a challenge to every pastor, leader, and believer around the world. It's time to bring the Church back in line with the message of the Gospel, to obey the great commission, and to follow the blueprint for the Church found in the Book of Acts!

For years now, pressure has been applied by the enemy to cause pastors and leaders to back down from the Word of God, producing a weak, religious "Church" that does not shake cities and nations. This book will stir you to re-read the Gospels and the Book of Acts and cry out for a Heaven-sent avalanche of Pentecostal power. The only hope for the nations and billions of those who don't know Jesus is for the Church to rise up and be the Church.

Allow this book to challenge you; may a God-given hunger cry develop so that you rise up and return to the simplicity of "God's Blueprint" laid out in His Word. It's time to preach God's Word with signs following and win the lost.

I salute Andy for contending and sticking his neck out to boldly proclaim these truths—Andy, keep up the good work. We are blessed by your ministry and what you are allowing God to do through you.

Dr. Rodney Howard-Browne,
Revival Ministries International
The River at Tampa Bay Church

The Church is central in God's plan to bring salvation to humanity. It's the one thing He would build and the thing He is coming back for. God intended His Church to be a way for people to see God's nature and character, and to experience His goodness and love. *God's Blueprint for His Church* will take you back to God's original purpose for His Church in a fresh and revealing way. Andy Elmes' book is an excellent resource and tool for everyone who wants to be part of building His Church.

Gary Clarke, Lead Pastor
Hillsong Church London

God's Blueprint for His Church is definitely a book for every church leader. I know Andy Elmes very well and consider him to be an experienced church pastor with a wealth of insight and understanding on church life today. Refreshing and enjoyable, the content will also deeply challenge and stir your heart for the Church of Jesus Christ. His Church is unquestionably the greatest organization on earth today. Designed by God as His masterpiece, it consists of and is shaped by ordinary people just like you and me. As you digest the wisdom in these pages, I pray that God will breathe His Spirit upon you, instilling fresh hope, faith, and dedication to Him, while loving and participating in His amazing Church.

Ashley Schmierer,
International President
Christian Outreach Centre Churches

About 13 years ago in Portsmouth I met and later preached for a dynamic young man of God, Andy Elmes. He had vitality, a sense of God's anointing, an infectious grin, and an intense passion brewing within. Recently, I was preaching again at his powerful growing church. Each day he met me with the same words: "I've been up writing this book into the early hours; it is consuming me." We talked of his passion to see God's Church restored to the unity, power, and dynamic spiritual leadership of the first-century church. Andy wasn't just writing a book; with God, he was wrestling through thoughts and ideas that will see the blueprint established for the next great phase of transformation in the Body of Christ. Andy has seen a strong, impacting church established under his leadership. He is raising great leaders under him. He is in heavy demand as one of the UK's most impacting and anointed speakers. He also ministers extensively globally. Yet he is so very far from satisfied. This book is a powerful statement of Andy's gut-wrenching passion for us to move from leadership to a place of spiritual leadership that will bring the Body of Christ into the place where our cities and nations shake under the hand of God. This book is brutally honest and has come from intense periods of intimacy with God. It will impact your life.

Tim Hall,
International Evangelist

CONTENTS

INTRODUCTION

I t was a Sunday morning, and I was sitting looking at the healthy-sized crowd we had attracted over the last 14 years of "doing church." We had started with twelve people, and now we represented a crowd across our congregations of well over a thousand. I should have been the happiest man in the world, right? I *was* happy, but something inside of me was aggravated. I looked across the crowd of good people and started to ask myself certain questions to locate the reason for my discomfort: *I have a crowd, but is a crowd what I want? Who is in the crowd? What difference is the crowd having on my city and beyond? Is the crowd consumer-based—only coming when we make it convenient, eating spoon-fed truth but leaving unchanged? Is this what God wants the Church to look like? Are we empowering and mobilizing God's people to be effective ministers in their world, or have we resorted to mere people storage?*

With these questions, a journey of rediscovery began that caused me to rethink the purpose of the Church on the earth. This journey would cause me to question how I was leading and what I was actually building. Was it the Church that Jesus wanted? Many months were spent thinking, asking questions, getting answers, and developing convictions and new persuasions. In the process, I joyfully rediscovered the original blueprint for the Church Jesus wants and have recommitted my life to building that. The amazing thing is that the answer was there all the time.

Let us take a moment together to dare to gaze at the blueprint He rolled out 2000 years ago; let us blow the dust off of it and talk about the great commission, discipleship, and what place the power of God has in 21st-century churches. Let us ask ourselves, "When we roll out the blueprint we currently have for 'building the Church,' does it look the same as His? Or have we added conservatories and extensions to it—that in themselves are not wrong, but may have distracted us from building that which He desires built?"

I have written this book to be provocative, challenging, and thought provoking. My desire is that it will act as itching powder down the back of the 21st-century Body of Christ to provoke us to answer honest questions that need to be revisited in our generation. As we rise to these challenges, I believe we can cause a spiritual shift in the Church—a return to the pattern for a Church that could once again seriously impact our nations as Jesus first intended for it to do.

This is what the Lord of Heaven's Armies says:
"The people are saying, 'The time has not yet come
to rebuild the house of the Lord.' Then the Lord sent
this message through the prophet Haggai:
'Why are you living in luxurious houses
while my house lies in ruins?
This is what the Lord of Heaven's Armies says:
Look at what's happening to you!
You have planted much but harvest little.
You eat but are not satisfied.
You drink but are still thirsty.
You put on clothes but cannot keep warm.
Your wages disappear as though you were putting them
in pockets filled with holes!
This is what the Lord of Heaven's Armies says:
Look at what's happening to you!
Now go up into the hills, bring down timber,
and rebuild my house. Then I will take pleasure in it
and be honored, says the Lord.
You hoped for rich harvests, but they were poor.
And when you brought your harvest home, I blew it away.
Why? Because my house lies in ruins,
says the Lord of Heaven's Armies,
while all of you are busy building your own fine houses'"
(Haggai 1:2-9).

1

WHO IS BUILDING WHAT?

*And I tell you that you are Peter, and on this rock I will **build** My **church**, and the gates of Hades will not overcome it* (Matthew 16:18 NIV).

We live in very interesting times—times when so many of the things that people have trusted in are suddenly failing them. People are searching for what offers certainty and security, but does not fail. They look for real answers to the real questions that they have. One of these questions is the timeless one that has been asked in different ways by different people through all generations: "Is there a God, and if so, what has He got to do with me?"

This is actually the most important question that we can ask. We need to be aware that today there are many counterfeits to the Church of Jesus in the marketplace of public opinion—each of them daily peddling every kind of deception and alternative philosophy imaginable, and each making the claim to be the telling the truth. These modern-day charlatans only make already-confused seekers even more confused. They also make it extremely difficult for the real Church with real answers to be heard amongst their crafty lies and deceptive offers, as they gently assure the seeker that all roads lead to the same place and same God. The 21st-century Church has a massive job to do, and that job is to make Jesus and His saving grace known to these people who are desperately seeking the truth concerning who God is.

The second most common set of questions I experience when I talk to people about God concern the Church: "What is the Church?" "What is the point or purpose of it in the world today?" Sadly, I think that some of the confusion is the result of churches who do not themselves know their own identity or purpose in the world. If they don't know these answers, then how on earth can they answer with conviction the questions being asked by a generation who earnestly seeks to know?

When I talk to un-churched people, it is not long before it surfaces that they actually do not have much of a problem with God; their problem is more often with the Church and how it has represented and sought to reveal God to them. I am sure that you have also experienced this on more than one occasion. Let's face it; God has certainly managed to keep His reputation far better than the Church has managed to keep theirs. But there is still time to turn this around if we have courageous hearts to do so. But before we go out there declaring who we are and what we are here to do, it is vital that we have a *revelation* concerning His Church, who we really are on the earth, and what we have been anointed and appointed by God to do.

BACK TO BASICS

The opening verse to this chapter is taken from that moment in Matthew 16 when Jesus asks Peter a very specific question. Prior to this question, Jesus had asked a general one of all the people who stood nearby that day: "Who do people say that I am?" The people standing around Him answered in what I call a "Google fashion." It was like they had typed His name into a Google search box, and then repeated what came up on the screen. Some of the people said this and some said that; some said Elijah and others said a prophet. All of their answers were probably based on what they had heard from others concerning His identity. Then He turned and asked for a personal response from His disciples, "What about you? Who am I to you?"

At that moment Peter stepped forward and said those incredible words, "You are the Christ, the Messiah, the anointed one. Jesus, You are God's Son." Jesus responded, "Flesh and blood did not give you this understanding [that's not a Google response, Peter], but My Father in Heaven revealed this to you" (see Matt. 16:13-17). Peter knew Jesus by revelation, and it was because of that revelation of Jesus that he was able to face the extreme things that came later in his life. Mere head knowledge certainly would not have kept Him strong enough or persuaded enough for what lay ahead.

In its truest, purest reality, Christianity is simply a personal relationship with a living God. It is not a religion or a bunch of ceremonies or legalistic expectancies. It's about a person. It's about knowing Him, knowing Jesus. Take the Christ out of Christianity, and all you are left with is "ianity," which leads to insanity. People start getting bored, weird, and stupid. They begin adding things and other philosophies that should never be added while continually losing sight of *Who* it's all really about.

Here's some good advice: let Jesus ever remain the central figure of your Christianity, and you will never go far wrong. I love to read the writings of Paul because the continual thread of his love and passion for the person of Jesus runs through them. I love it when he proclaims "let Jesus receive all the pre-eminence" in Colossians 1:18. What was he saying? Simply, to let Him (Jesus) always remain first—the very center of all we are and endeavor to do. When we allow Jesus to remain enthroned in His rightful place and daily feed on His words of truth, grace, and life, then our lives and the churches we build will always retain great health and vibrancy.

So if Jesus is the main thing, then we must love what He loves and hate what He hates. Equally, we need to be passionate about building what He is passionate about building. The Church He desires to build needs to be the Church that we are daily passionately committed to building—not an alternative one that we prefer or think may work better. It needs to be the Church that He wants and desires!

Two thousand years ago when Jesus declared that He would build His Church, He rolled out a blueprint of what the Church was meant to be upon the tabletop of His divine intentions. That is the blueprint I believe God is calling us back to today. That was the blueprint that the first Church committed to, and it is the pattern they handed to us to build by also. A blueprint is an interesting document with all its measurements, lines, and figures. Even when it is not yet built, it represents the specifics of a building complete in every way. To the untrained eye, it is just lines and numbers on a large page, but to the eye of the architect or owner, it represents the exact dimensions and instructions to building the house that is desired in their heart.

Remember, *we* do not build the Church, and we certainly did not start the building of it. Our opening text clearly says that Jesus builds the Church, and we have the honor of laboring and partnering with Him in its construction and advancement in our generation. It is good for us to remember the fact that His blueprint for the Church is the blueprint we are called to build by and not an adapted one that we think will work better, look nicer, or be more iconic. I feel that God is speaking to leaders, church builders, and believers to build effective and dynamic churches all across the earth today. He is calling His builders, His people, to return to the blueprint for a Church that will change the world.

When we take a moment to look at His blueprint for the Church and blow off the dust that we may have allowed to gather on it, we discover that we have all added a few things to it over the years; we have all put a few extensions and conservatories on the original building Jesus desired. By "extensions," I mean projects or things that spring from our individual desires and persuasions of what an effective church must look like and do. I don't mean this to be negative. These add-ons are often very good and cause the Church to have greater impact in new and different ways—unless our focus and energy is consumed by the additions rather than the central, fundamental thing that Jesus wants built. Our extensions and conservatories then become merely fashionable distractions; we may feel fulfilled and contented by them, but does He?

We are living in crucial times when the Church has a great opportunity to shine, but we must make sure that the Church we are building in the 21st century still carries the DNA of the Church Jesus first put on the blueprint when He said, "I will build My Church." We must remain committed to being relevant 21st-century churches with an uncompromised 1st-century vision, building according to the pattern handed to us by the apostles and prophets of the faith—many of whom gave their lives to construct its everlasting, never-failing foundations. It is also good to remind ourselves at this point that, while its foundations have been laid by apostles and prophets, its chief cornerstone is and must always be Christ Jesus Himself.

> *Consequently, you are no longer foreigners and strangers, but fellow citizens with God's people and also members of His household, built on the foundation of the apostles and prophets, with Christ Jesus Himself as the chief cornerstone. In Him the whole building is joined together and rises to become a holy temple in the Lord* (Ephesians 2:19-21 NIV).

AVOIDING DISTRACTIONS

Let's be honest, when it comes to the modern-day Church, especially in western nations, there have been far too many distractions in the last few years; we certainly do not need any more. Distractions have come from every possible and imaginable direction; in some places, distractions have caused Christianity to become downright bizarre, while in other places something that is non-effective but highly fashionable—offering prestige, fame, fortune, and great opportunities to people who never would have normally had them outside of the ministry. Now, they step into the spotlight of fame and prominence daily, expounding on subjects like prosperity and the giving of your money in ways that are far beyond what the Bible ever set out for us to teach. Before long, these same people find their lives being driven more by personal agendas and shady motives than good old-fashioned godly calling, which finds its strength in selflessness.

Please do not hear what I am not saying. I believe in prosperity and godly increase. I believe as it says in Jeremiah that God has plans to prosper as well as to give a future and a hope (see Jer. 29:11). However, when prosperity becomes the end goal and the central theme to all that a person preaches, it can become the very ugliest of things to watch or encounter and a very dangerous distraction to the soul of a man. Prosperity is not in itself a destination; it is always at its best when it has a purpose and a cause to serve, and there remains no better cause to serve than Jesus the King and His Kingdom extended throughout the earth.

Also, thanks to the speedy development of modern-day media, we now get to flick on our televisions and watch godly programs any time we want. What a resource we have in our modern world! It's great to sit and hear preachers of truth who teach from God-given revelation and who disciple and enlarge the life of the listening believer. I am sure you will also agree that it is equally frustrating to hear some of the other preachers, who obviously do not yet know how to rightly divide the Word of truth, standing on platforms before TV cameras, taking biblical truths and godly principles to the extreme. Scriptures and doctrines are regularly taken out of their context, often once again to support out-of-balance prosperity-based messages. Don't get me wrong. There are many fine leaders who minister healthy truth across these media outlets by day and by night for Kingdom advancement, but there are also others who are not called to do it. Instead, they just paid their way on and don't realize that they are actually guilty of confusing people more than leading them in the pathways of godly life. If only there was some sort of apostolic governing body to both monitor and filter the programming being broadcast to a world that desperately needs Jesus.

On a side note, this is why I believe it's still vitally important and wise that every Christian be planted in a healthy, local church with a Spirit-filled pastor who knows the Bible. When things are heard that do not sound quite right, they can be talked about, rightly divided, and checked out so they are not just innocently swallowed, causing spiritual indigestion. Paul actually taught that we are not to "heap" up teachers because of having "itching ears" (see 2 Tim. 4:3-4). He also endorsed the need for having fathers in the faith, not just a multitude of instructors (see 1 Cor. 4:14-16). There is certainly a multitude available today with all the media that is readily accessible. We need to be careful that we don't just feast on every opinion being preached, but rather that we hunger and pursue truth—and that we have the maturity to rightly divide the Word in a way that is effective.

Other modern-day distractions can be as simple as "brick and mortar"—when Church builders and believers get so distracted by the maintenance and the construction of physical buildings that they forget to put the needed effort into building the actual Church of Jesus Christ, which is the people. Some get distracted by the successes that can come with modern Christianity, and without knowing it, slowly cross over from building God's Kingdom to building and financing their own. I could continue on with the many other distractions that face the 21st-century Church, but I am sure you are just as aware of them as I am. Church, it's a new day. I believe God is sending out a call to His Church across the earth: "Enough distractions, extensions, and conservatories. Return to the blueprint; build again the Church I want built, and build it according to the designs I originally gave." Once again, I believe we need to look at His blueprint soberly and have the passion and courage to underline what He has underlined, emphasize what He has emphasized, and build to the scale and shape that He desires.

JOIN ME AT THE ARCHITECT'S TABLE

So let's consider that first blueprint by which the early Church built. Let's consider how its ancient lines affect and determine what we are building today in our generation. Let us dare to blow away the dust that may have gathered as we got distracted. Let us make the decision to stop trying to overlay it with our own blueprints of what we prefer; rather, let us look at it with fresh eyes and a hunger to build what He desires. Take time to evaluate again with the help of God's Spirit what the great Architect Jesus first saw and desired when He opened the door to that first Church that was born in fire. May we be moved again to build according to the pattern! As we dare to look again at a number of key verses found in the end of the Gospels, the Book of Acts, and beyond, may we again discover the foundations and dimensions of what we are called to build. In this book, we will pilgrimage together rediscovering the things that Jesus and the early Church focused on and were passionate about. We will ask honest questions to gain fresh revelations concerning what that is which He still loves and has committed to build.

We will also ask some brave questions along the way concerning where we stand today with the great commission, among other things. Are we sending and mobilizing people, or are we just fashionable storage units for satisfied overfed saints, intent on remaining consumers and not becoming the consumed? Does the word "Go" in the great commission inspire and excite us to burst out beyond the walls and make a difference in the world, or have we conveniently changed that great commission from "Go into all the world" to a much simpler and easier "Go to church"? Are we guilty of treating the Great Commission more like a great suggestion, no longer moved by the people-loving passion in the One who originally gave the charge?

And when it comes to our going, do we make disciples and see people supernaturally transformed by the Spirit and the Word; or do we settle for getting people nebulously saved—leaving them as new-borns without the understanding of who they now are and what they now have because of the perfect and finished work of Jesus?

How about the power of God—that raw, life-changing force that turns confused and broken lives right side up? Where does that fit in the fashionable, safe churches we have built? In our endeavors to keep people from weird, wacky, and spooky things, are we also keeping them from understanding the life-changing dimension of the Spirit? Are we putting as much value on the Person and the Power of the Holy Spirit as Jesus and the first apostles did? How about other things the early Church made a priority in the early chapters of Acts— things like being devoted to the apostles' doctrine? Are we loving the truth as they did—or are we trying to make it fit the convenient life we now choose to live? Are we devoted to each other with a divine, selfless passion, and to the breaking of bread and prayer? What place does faith have today in our lives and in the Church? Are we concerned that Jesus find faith when He returns to earth, or are we developing our capacity to be reasonable people doing reasonable things that take no faith?

These are the questions I want to stir, aggravate, and even irritate you with for the purpose of stirring a return to the blueprint. Lay aside any preconceived ideas and hang-ups. Join me on an honest journey fueled by desire to rediscover the design for the Church that Jesus wants us to build for Him in our very needy generation.

BUILDING ACCORDING TO THE PATTERN

So what do I mean when I say that we are to build according to the pattern? Simply that God is never without a plan. He always has a plan for what He wants to build or do. He gives us the plan, and we are to build according to it. This is what happened in the Old Testament concerning the construction of the tabernacle. Man did not come up with the pattern for a tabernacle that God would like. God came up with it, and then handed it to man to construct for Him. I believe it works in the same way with the New Testament Church. Jesus has handed us a pattern of what He wants, and as we read through the New Testament, we can see clearly His designs. As with the temple and tabernacle in the Old Testament, He has left nothing out.

Throughout the New Testament, He speaks of its values, its government, its purpose, and so much more. It's all there in the blueprint of Scripture He has given to us. When God wanted the tabernacle made, He spoke to Moses precisely about its materials and furnishings. All Moses had to do was mobilize his team to build it according to the blueprint that God had provided. As you read through the verses that follow, you soon notice that God is a God of great detail. He gave the patterns for the lampstands and even the smallest ornamental parts of the tabernacle.

> Then have them make a sanctuary for Me, and I will dwell among them. Make this tabernacle and all its furnishings exactly like the **pattern** I will show you (Exodus 25:8-9 NIV).

> This is how the lampstand was made: It was made of hammered gold—from its base to its blossoms. The lampstand was made exactly like the **pattern** the LORD had shown Moses (Numbers 8:4 NIV).

Another verse that caught my attention when it came to God giving a pattern to Moses for what He wanted built was this one a bit further on in Exodus 25: "See that you make them according to the *pattern* shown you on the mountain" (Exod. 25:40 NIV).

We know that Moses' time alone with God on the mountain was a very personal time during which he received the blueprint for what God wanted built on the earth at that time. This again is a great type and shadow of the Church He wants built on the earth today. As with Moses, you do not find His pattern among the crowds and many opinions of men; you find it when you go and spend time in

His presence. As we dare to spend good time "up the mountain" or in His presence, then we too will come down with the pattern for the Church God wants built in this generation; and as with Moses, we too will have a blueprint that lacks no detail.

We also see this principle in the New Testament as twice it makes reference to the tabernacle being constructed in accordance with "the pattern" Moses received as he spent time in His presence on the mountain.

Our ancestors had the tabernacle of the covenant law with them in the wilderness. It had been made as God directed Moses, according to the **pattern** *he had seen* (Acts 7:44 NIV).

…who serve the copy and shadow of the heavenly things, as Moses was divinely instructed when he was about to make the tabernacle. For He said, "See that you make all things according to the **pattern** *shown you on the mountain"* (Hebrews 8:5).

In the Old Testament, we see how God wanted His physical tabernacle constructed. He did not leave it to the builder's imagination but gave precise instruction concerning what He wanted it to look like. This is for us now in the New Testament a great type and shadow of what He wants from us today. It is no longer a physical church He wants to build, but rather a spiritual one. In the same way, however, I believe He knows what He wants and has handed us a pattern through the hands of the apostles and generations of faithful church leaders; that pattern is contained within the pages of the Bible. Let's return to the pattern He has given so we may build Him the New Testament Church that He wants.

ABOUT SPIRITUAL CULTURE, NOT A NATURAL ONE

As we know, the Church of Jesus Christ opened its doors over two thousand years ago in a nation called Israel. Before we go any further, I want to clarify that when we talk about returning to the original 1st-century blueprint for the Church, I am talking about building according to the spiritual, not the natural. I am not referring to the national culture or values of Jerusalem or Israel, but to a spiritual blueprint built on the values and desires of God, a Kingdom culture that transcends all the natural cultures upon the earth.

I feel that if I do not take a moment to mention this, it could well bring an element of confusion rather than clarity by leaving you with certain unanswered questions, such as, "Are we then to go 'Israeli' or 'Jewish' in our thinking and daily outworking when building the Church that God wants?" "Do we need to look or act in some way like 1st-century Israeli Jews?" No, I don't believe this is what is needed at all. To believe this would be to completely miss the point of God's plan for a worldwide Church. Though we are to respect and pray for Israel as a nation and as a people, Israel was the national culture that the first Church was initially planted in—not the national culture that every local church be modeled on; the Church has spread to every nation, tribe, and tongue. Today, the Church needs to be built according to God's original spiritual blueprint, relevant to each and every culture in which it finds itself established.

For too many years we have watched an element of Christians who are Gentile by natural birth trying to imitate Jewish customs in a desperate endeavor to become something they feel they need to become to be fully accepted by God the Father. This error most often springs from a misunderstanding of the finished work of Christ which actually made the sheep (people) who were once of two separate pastures into the sheep (people) of one new pasture. It is the result of ignorance concerning the truths of the New Covenant (the final agreement between God and man) that declares that God has now taken two men (Jewish and Gentile) and made them one new man in Christ.

Therefore remember that you, once Gentiles in the flesh—who are called Uncircumcision by what is called the Circumcision made in the flesh by hands—that at that time you were without Christ, being aliens from the commonwealth of Israel and strangers from the covenants of promise, having no hope and without God in the world. But now in Christ Jesus you who once were far off have been brought near by the blood of Christ. For He Himself is our peace, who has made both one, and has broken down the middle wall of separation, having abolished in His flesh the enmity, that is, the law of commandments contained in ordinances, so as to create in Himself one new man from the two, thus making peace, and that He might reconcile them both to God in one body through the cross, thereby putting to death the enmity. And He came and preached peace to you who were afar off and to those who were near. For through Him we both have access by one Spirit to the Father. Now, therefore, you are no longer strangers and foreigners, but fellow citizens with the saints and members of the household of God (Ephesians 2:11-19).

These verses indicate clearly that for a Gentile to spend his time trying to be Jewish is actually a dead work (a pointless endeavor). In doing so, he disregards what was so wonderfully achieved by Jesus at the cross in removing these natural divides that once separated us but separate us no longer. The reality is that it is faith in the complete and finished work of Jesus that produces the required righteousness that pleases God and leaves a man, whether he is a Jew by first birth or a Gentile standing complete in Him. To do justice to these truths would take a book in itself. It is sufficient to say that the New Testament recognizes that our salvation is the result of God qualifying us and not our national birth or our own performance; we simply receive by faith the gift of righteousness and the abundance of His grace freely given by Him to all who believe.

> *For it is by grace you have been saved, through faith—and this is not from yourselves, it is the gift of God—not by works, so that no one can boast* (Ephesians 2:8-9 NIV).

If we are going to live from a New Covenant perspective, we must understand that all the dividing walls have now been removed and our citizenship is of one spiritual Kingdom independent of our national culture or place of birth. We must also understand that access into this citizenship is by faith alone; inside of this Kingdom all stand with the same benefits joined to the same root (see Rom. 11), fully paid for and redeemed by the blood of Jesus.

> *There is neither Jew nor Gentile, neither slave nor free, nor is there male and female, for you are all one in Christ Jesus. If you belong to Christ, then you are Abraham's seed, and heirs according to the promise* (Galatians 3:28-29 NIV).

It is important to establish these truths because so often those who earnestly try to build the Church to look and feel like the natural culture of Israel do not realize that God wants us to build His Church according to a spiritual culture and pattern, producing churches that are relevant and effective in every single place they operate—whether it be the Middle East, Europe, or Asia. There is now one Church with one King where all are welcome and accepted when they enter in by faith and grace.

The Church has many sounds and many styles, each representing the nations that they are located within and the people they are reaching, yet each being built according to the common spiritual blueprint that supersedes any one national way of doing things. I have travelled the nations with the Gospel and actually enjoy the natural cultural differences in churches in different parts of the world. I love the individual uniqueness of the churches in the nations—yet they all worship and serve the same King. Allow me to emphasize that I love Israel and God's plans for the Jewish people and that nation. I have had the privilege to minister to believers there on a number of occasions, but I am also aware that God has called me to build His Church primarily within the shores of Great Britain and Europe. So when you look to build His Church with Him, you have to purpose to build according to the spiritual culture of His blueprint in a way that is relevant, yet not watered down—a Church that speaks the truth concerning who He is and what He has done in a language that the locals in your area can understand, receive, and apply.

2

IT'S TIME FOR ALIGNMENT

*And He is the head of the body, the church, who is the begin-
ning, the firstborn from the dead, that in all things He may
have the preeminence* (Colossians 1:18).

HAVING A CORRECT PERCEPTION

We have established now that it is vital that we have a clear, God-
given revelation of the Church, not just of God. Your perception
of the Church will always determine both how you choose to
relate to it and what you are willing to do for it. Think about how your
perception of God affects how you relate to Him on a daily basis.

If you have no personal experience of a relationship with Him and
have just been handed an image by religious-minded people, then you
may well see Him as unapproachable and unloving when this is so
far from the actual truth of who He is. Alternatively, maybe you were
raised by a father who was abusive in some way and you have a personal stock room of many bad memories concerning being fathered.

One day someone says to you, "Your Father in Heaven loves you," and instead of that statement bringing the intended smile, it actually causes you to respond in a more fearful or cautious way. Can you see how your earthly experience of a father could greatly affect your perception of God as a heavenly Father and cause you to want to run from Him rather than run to Him—or, when you consider His face, to see a scowl of disappointment instead of eyes filled with adoring delight? The cure for this perception problem is to allow God's Spirit to reveal to you, through His Word, who God the Father really is, and as you gain a revelation (revealed knowledge) of Him, suddenly the way you desire to respond to Him will very naturally become completely different.

In the same way, how you see, judge, or perceive the Church will determine how you relate to it, the place it has in your life, and the position it takes on your personal priority chart. So, how do we know the Church as we should? By its historical reputation or by how others have revealed her to us? This is certainly not the best or wisest way, especially when you see some people around today doing crazy things and calling themselves the Church—or when you encounter a lifeless, ineffective temple of guilt and condemnation where you go in feeling great and come out an hour later feeling like rubbish.

No, to truly know the Church correctly and to see it in all of its beauty you need to turn to the blueprint that is contained in His Word and then let the Spirit of God show you how wonderful and glorious it really is. The New Testament refers frequently to the Church by a number of different descriptive titles, each one revealing another facet of its God-given identity and purpose. It is good for us to have a healthy understanding concerning these individual facets or revelations. I want to discuss two of these descriptive titles for His Church, in particular.

HIS CHURCH IS THE BRIDE OF JESUS

Wives, submit to your own husbands, as to the Lord. For the husband is head of the wife, as also Christ is head of the church;

and He is the Saviour of the body. Therefore, just as the church is subject to Christ, so let the wives be to their own husbands in everything. Husbands, love your wives, just as Christ also loved the church and gave Himself for her, that He might sanctify and cleanse her with the washing of water by the word, that He might present her to Himself a glorious church, not having spot or wrinkle or any such thing, but that she should be holy and without blemish. So husbands ought to love their own wives as their own bodies; he who loves his wife loves himself. For no one ever hated his own flesh, but nourishes and cherishes it, just as the Lord does the church. For we are members of His body, of His flesh and of His bones. "For this reason a man shall leave his father and mother and be joined to his wife, and the two shall become one flesh." This is a great mystery, but I speak concerning Christ and the church (Ephesians 5:22-32).

HIS CHURCH IS THE HOUSEHOLD OF GOD

Now, therefore, you are no longer strangers and foreigners, but fellow citizens with the saints and members of the household of God (Ephesians 2:19).

Both of these titles reveal that the Church is actually not a cold and unapproachable building or priesthood but rather a relational, living community. In these two examples, we see Him refer to us as His Bride and His household, belonging to and being a part of Him. I want to underscore that in choosing examples to reveal His Church, He chose relational not religious descriptions; both have connotations of intimacy, revealing that the Church is something that He cares deeply about and for.

Throughout the New Testament, the Church is referred to symbolically as His temple, His army, His field, and indeed, His master plan for changing the world. But the one metaphor I want to focus in on joins us to Him in a closer way than any of the others: the Church, according to the Bible, is His Body. Clearly, this metaphor reveals that, in His perspective, He is the head, and we are His Body; there is a divine union between the Church (us) and Him.

> *For as we have many members in one body, but all the members do not have the same function, so we, being many, are one body in Christ, and individually members of one another* (Romans 12:4-5).

REVIVAL OR REFORMATION?

Revival is one of those Christian "in" words that people love to use. Often, they attach the word to the moving of God's Spirit in a certain context. When we take a moment to look at it through that particular lens, the truth is that we are actually constantly experiencing revival, as God's Spirit is constantly moving even when we are not. More often than not, revival is used to describe a set of meetings being put on by believers where they concentrate on pressing into God and seeing His Spirit move in power. I love the thought that our God revives, and I fully believe that He does; I just get a little bit annoyed when I hear it used so often for "what our nation needs."

Revival can be quite a nebulous term; it can mean many things to different people with regard to the movement of the Holy Spirit and what that should look like, but when it comes to what will change our nation long-term, personally, I am not sure if it is the right word to use. Please bear in mind that this is being written by a guy who spent a lot of his early years in ministry, travelling and holding revivals and crusades all over the world. Indeed, I still preach at revival-type meetings around the world and love to see people press in to God and get a touch from Him. But here I am talking about the bigger picture of what will really change our cities and nations, especially in the West where we have seen so much, been to so much, and bought every book, CD, and T-shirt that was for sale at all the events we have all flooded to over the last few years. Though these events have been inspirational and empowering, I do not believe we have yet seen the citywide or nationwide impact that God intends for His Church to have in this generation; neither do I think that we have really seen what we should have seen for the time, money, and energy we have spent both on them and in them.

Have the revivals and conferences we have known up to now produced a mobilized army that is sold out, equipped, and unstoppable— an army that God is able to use to bring a release of His Spirit that causes the Church to reap the desired harvest in the nations? Will people gathering in prayer closets, praying for revival, really be what will cause the world to be impacted by God's Spirit? Or do we, as well as praying, need to get some of that good old Book-of-Acts courage that came with the speaking in tongues and the appearance of spiritual drunkenness, and get up and be the witnesses (and the Church) that God needs us to be to our generation? Just maybe, the word we are looking for is not so much *revival* but *reformation*. Some would argue that revival *brings* reformation; I think that, actually, reformation is more likely to be the railway track by which revival comes into a nation.

So, what do I mean by reformation? The most basic definition of the word means to re-form or to re-shape. Reformation happens when something takes on a new or "reformed" shape. I honestly believe that this is the moment that is at hand for the Church; it's time for the Church across the western world to re-shape, not necessarily into something completely new that has never been seen, but actually into something old, something original. I believe it's time for the Church to re-shape itself so that we might look and sound like Jesus and that first Church He opened in the Book of Acts.

Think about it, the Bible says He is the Head; we are the Body. Surely the Head and the Body should look, sound, and feel the same, regardless of whatever culture or generation they find themselves living in, right?

And He put all things under His feet, and gave Him to be head over all things to the church (Ephesians 1:22).

For the husband is head of the wife, as also Christ is head of the church; and He is the Savior of the body (Ephesians 5:23).

And He is the head of the body, the church, who is the beginning, the firstborn from the dead, that in all things He may have the preeminence (Colossians 1:18).

IT'S TIME TO ALIGN

It's time to put an end to what I term *Frankenstein Christianity*, a type or style of Christianity that causes the world to daily experience a different body and head when they encounter God and His Church. It may be simplistic on my part, but I believe when people meet us, the Church, it should be like meeting Him, the Head. We need to remember that we represent Him and everything He stands for. Look at this next verse: "Love has been perfected among us in this: that we may have boldness in the day of judgment; *because as He is, so are we in this world*" (1 John 4:17).

Think about that: as He is, so are we in this world. This speaks of our spiritual standing, authority, and the rights we now have as we walk on this earth because of His perfect work on our behalf. But what if we were to turn this verse around? What if we were to look at this verse in the context of us representing Him? What if we were to say, "As we are on the earth, so is He in Heaven"?

I'm not changing the Scripture—just asking if it works just as strongly when we turn it around this way. I think it does. I think it leaves us with another great challenge. As we live our lives here on the earth, calling ourselves the Church, His Body, we cause the people who daily encounter us to perceive what He is like in Heaven. Imagine that: people will estimate and evaluate who He is by watching or encountering us on a daily basis. There is no doubt they will. I wonder how many never got to meet, or wanted to meet, the wonderful Savior, Jesus, because they met people calling themselves His Body (His representatives) who had stinking attitudes or religious hang-ups that actually made Him, the one seated in Heaven, undesirable?

This is a sobering thought. As we live out our lives *here*, so people judge Him to be over *there*. Let us make sure that there is indeed an alignment between Body and Head, and that when they encounter us, they get a true glimpse and feel of Him. When they encounter His Body on the earth, they should get a taste of how incredible, loving, and life-filled He, the Head, is. Imagine how sad it would be if someone who had been in my church for forty years was to die at a ripe old age, go to Heaven, bump into Jesus on the streets of gold, and say, "Who are You?" How sad for this one not to recognize Him after living with His Body for so long.

We need to make sure that our 21st-century churches look and feel like their Head and owner, Jesus. Now, this affects all sorts of things that we do on a daily basis, and the implications and outworkings are not only spiritual but also very practical, including the simplest of things like how we run our welcome teams at our church events.

CHURCH WELCOME

If you are on the church welcome team, you need to realize what an important job you have. You are most often the first point of contact for people coming to your church for the first time; that's a big responsibility. Think about it, they are going to make their first assumption of what your church is like by your welcome. Let me make it worse for you: for many, their first experience of God will be the welcome they get from you as they step into God's house.

I believe our welcome should always be incredible. Again, let's relate this to the whole theme of Head and Body alignment. Close your eyes and imagine what it would have been like to meet Jesus personally on the streets of Jerusalem two thousand years ago. Do you think you would have felt accepted or condemned by His smile and the warmth of His greeting? I believe you would have felt so welcomed and accepted it would have taken you a lifetime to get over it. Remember, John 3:17 says that Jesus did not come to condemn but to save. He gave out such a welcome, people never wanted to leave, and He had to get His team to come up with feeding programs for the crowds because they would not go home!!

If He never condemned people coming to Him, what right does the Church have to take the role of judge and jury with regard to people coming or returning to God's house? Who are we to make people feel any less welcome than Jesus would?

I love the account of the return of the younger son in the parable of the wayward child that Jesus shared (see Luke 15:11-32). In that parable, He made many points, using each of the three leading characters—the father, the son, and the older brother—to do so. In one of the final lessons of the parable, He speaks of how the older brother welcomed the repentant younger brother back. The older brother had a stinking attitude and was judgmental and accusing, thinking he knew more than he actually did. The father turned and rebuked him for not having a spirit of celebration for the son who had returned.

We need to make sure that we don't have that "ugly brother" syndrome when people are "coming home" even if, like the older brother, we know where they have been and what they have been up to. Any inside knowledge we may have does not give us the right to reject or condemn anyone coming or returning to God's house.

In Family Church, we spend time training our welcome teams and hosts to treat people just as Jesus would. This is very important because, often when we speak to first-time visitors after a few weeks, most of them comment on how welcome they felt and how easy we made it for them to step over the scary threshold of the church. These days, I work a lot at helping churches to be the best they can be; often it comes down to some of these smaller things, not the larger things they think need change. Remember, Song of Solomon says it's the little foxes that spoil the vine (see Song 2:15); lack of care and excellence with the small things can be what chiefly hinders what you are trying to build.

I remember having a Sunday off a couple of years back; I was at a point in my life when I was really praying for God to give me a specific answer for some situations I was facing. Then, just as He told Jeremiah to go to the potter's house to learn something (see Jer. 18:2), I felt God telling me to go to a specific, small church nearby where I lived.

Being on holiday—and still being immersed in Family Church culture—I went as I was, wearing my shorts and T-shirt; all of my tattoos from my "before Christ" days were on display like an art exhibition simply because it was a very hot day. OK, I must admit I probably did not look like a pastor when I walked into the church that afternoon, but should that have mattered? When I walked in, I noticed about twelve people whom I soon realized were the normal Sunday night group. I was smiled at and sheepishly greeted by a lovely, older man, but no one else really introduced themselves or wanted to know who I was. I was left to find somewhere to sit by myself and was looked at through the corner of most other eyes—to check I was not doing drugs or stealing something, I suppose. To tell you the truth, I felt really unwelcome.

It was the communion service, and, as they got ready to serve the bread and wine, I noticed, three times, a warning was given not to take the bread and wine in an unfitting way. All three times, the man leading communion looked at me when he said it. When it came by, I took the bread and the wine with a confident smile, from the cautious hand of the server, leaving him slightly confused.

I remember thinking, *God, why did You send me here? Are You having a laugh?* Then, during the message, the preacher turned to a verse in the Bible that answered the question I had asked God earlier that day in such a specific way that it was beyond normal. I got so excited as the Scripture was read; it was *rhema* to my spirit, and I was grateful

God had sent me to that church to speak to me the Word I needed for the situations I was facing.

But to tell you the truth, I was not grateful for how I had felt as I sat there all alone. I felt isolated, judged, even unwanted; the crazy thing is, those precious people are probably praying for people to come and for revival each week. Let's make sure the way we welcome people, as the Body of Christ, is the same as the welcome they would get from the Head if they met Him, lest we find ourselves being more like Frankenstein than Jesus.

MANIFESTATION OF POWER

When I continue to ponder on what people would have experienced when they encountered Jesus two thousand years ago, another obvious example that comes to mind is power. They would have encountered power coming from Him that turned things around, that set them free from things that had held them captive. When people meet us, when they come to our church, do they experience power—or just sympathy, counseling, and a heartfelt "there, there…"? Again, if the Head has power, then the Body should have power—unless the Body does not know that it's connected to the Head.

In these days, when so many strive to be seeker-friendly to increase numbers, we must be sure that we do not deny that we are a people of power. We are not merely an organization but a spiritual organism (I will share more on this in the chapter on spiritual leadership). Today, God still wants to release His power through His Body to meet the needs of people just as He released His power through His natural body two thousand years ago.

I know we have to make church a safe place for people to come to, but we are not called to make it a non-supernatural place in doing so. As I said before, the issue really is to protect people from the "weird and spooky," not from the manifest power of God. Also, when making the church a place that is both safe and supernatural for people, we need to look at what day we are living in.

Often, it is when we try to imitate what the supernatural looked like and sounded like in the old days that we get into trouble. We need to be committed to being supernaturally "current." For example, prophecy no longer requires you to stand on a stage with a quivering voice, declaring, "Thus says the Lord!" Such a statement removes people's right to judge for themselves. You can be a whole lot nicer than that in your delivery and lose none of the power. The early Church moved in the power of God's Spirit and knew how to use the gifts of the Spirit; they experienced the supernatural on a daily basis. If we are building by the same blueprint, then we too must be a place where God's power is experienced by the people who come—a place where we are not hiding the dimension of the Spirit from people but helping them to experience, understand, and enter into it for themselves. If the Head is powerful, then the Body needs to be powerful too.

LIFE

There are many other examples and analogies I could use to speak of the need for alignment between the Head and the Body, but I believe you get the gist of what I am saying. You may even be thinking of other examples relevant for yourself. But I do believe another vital, nonnegotiable attribute for us to have in common is *life*. The Church must be a place that is full of life and releases life at every opportunity. We are not called to represent death; hopefully, you do not believe that when the tomb closed after Jesus was buried, it was all over. But if you do, I have some great news: it never ended there! On the third day, Jesus rose from the dead with resurrection life and became the firstfruits of all those who would be saved (us). So often when we talk about Jesus, we speak of Him forgiving or making payment for our sins, which is true, but what is also true is that He made us alive; He caused us to be born again and raised to newness of life with Him.

And you, being dead in your trespasses and the uncircumcision of your flesh, He has made alive together with Him, having forgiven you all trespasses (Colossians 2:13).

But God, who is rich in mercy, because of His great love with which He loved us, even when we were dead in trespasses, made us alive together with Christ (by grace you have been saved) (Ephesians 2:4-5).

Therefore we were buried with Him through baptism into death, that just as Christ was raised from the dead by the glory of the Father, even so we also should walk in newness of life (Romans 6:4).

The thief does not come except to steal, and to kill, and to destroy. I have come that they may have life, and that they may have it more abundantly (John 10:10).

HE HAS MADE US ALIVE, TOGETHER WITH HIM!

Just as the Spirit raised Him to life, so has He raised us to life, and it is this life that we are to manifest to a dead world. It is the fragrance of His life in our lives that will attract and draw people to Him, not the smell and sound of death. It's amazing, when you begin to look through the New Testament, how many times the word *life* is mentioned. If you study the context each time it is mentioned, before long, you begin to see that the Gospel (good news) of Jesus is all about life. That being the fact, His Church (His Body on the earth) should ooze life out of every pore of its being. When people meet us as a group and as individuals, they should encounter life as they never have before. They have wandered through a life that offers mere happiness—and not the life and joy that comes from a living God!

Church should be a life experience. From the moment they come through the door, people should experience it. Everything that comes from the platform or stage should carry it; the atmosphere should be filled with it. Life! I have told my musicians never to stand still and sing but to demonstrate and manifest life as they praise and worship. Who gives a rip about being British? This is for the King of kings.

The Bible says everything in creation responds to God: the trees of the field clap their hands; the mountains and waves declare His majesty; everything celebrates Him (except, perhaps, some British Christians). Well, it's time to change that. We need to raise a generation that knows how to respond to God in praise and worship with passion and enthusiasm, a people who love to worship Him, unashamed in Spirit and in truth! I am not referring to the style or type of music used for praise and worship, rather to the spirit of it. Is it carrying His life?

I have also told my team that if I ever make a mistake and accidently invite someone to speak who gets up on the stage and dribbles on with tales of woe, don't wait for my nod, pull them off by their legs! The stage should always be life-giving and a point of contact for the life of God, a place that gives nothing less than faith, hope, and belief.

THE HALLMARK OF GOD

I honestly believe that life is a hallmark of God. God evidences who He is using and what He is doing next with the hallmark of life. Think about one great example of this. Remember when God needed to appoint a high priest in the Book of Numbers? He needed to appoint a high priest, and that role meant a number of things. One of these was that the high priest was the voice of God to that generation; God would use the high priest to speak on His behalf to the people. There is a great account in the Book of Numbers concerning how He selected the first high priest. Take a look at how God identified, or hallmarked, him as the one He would use. At that time, a whole bunch of grumbling was going on concerning who should be in charge. God had a plan to get the issue straightened out.

The LORD said to Moses, "Speak to the Israelites and get twelve staffs from them, one from the leader of each of their ancestral tribes. Write the name of each man on his staff. On the staff of Levi write Aaron's name, for there must be one staff for the head of each ancestral tribe. Place them in the tent of meeting in front of the ark of the covenant law, where I meet with you. The staff belonging to the man I choose will sprout, and I will rid myself of this constant grumbling against you by the Israelites" (Numbers 17:1-5 NIV).

Each of the twelve tribes had a leader, and each leader thought he should be the voice of the people. So God gave Moses instructions, and the people did as He said. You can imagine each leader putting his staff into the tent and thinking, *It's me. I know it's me; they will all see when God picks me.* The next morning they all returned, and this is what happened:

The next day Moses entered the tent and saw that Aaron's staff, which represented the tribe of Levi, had not only sprouted but had budded, blossomed and produced almonds. Then Moses brought out all the staffs from the LORD's presence to all the Israelites. They looked at them, and each of the leaders took his own staff. The LORD said to Moses, "Put back Aaron's staff in front of the ark of the covenant law, to be kept as a sign to the rebellious. This will put an end to their grumbling against Me, so that they will not die." Moses did just as the LORD commanded him (Numbers 17: 8-11 NIV).

The next morning, it was suddenly obvious who God had chosen. There were eleven staffs on the ground, unchanged. But in the midst of them was Aaron's staff; it had changed dramatically overnight. It had sprouted, budded, blossomed, and produced ripe almonds. This dead stick had experienced the whole life cycle of a living tree overnight while in a tent with God's presence.

People must have been so amazed; they must have looked at it and asked, "How? How does something that was dead because of separation from its life source, live again?" They must have looked at it over and over to try to discover where it was getting its life from. The truth is they would never see with natural eyes, only spiritual ones. If they could have seen with spiritual vision, they would have seen it was connected to God. His life was causing resurrection life to flow through the staff, causing fruitfulness and harvest to be produced from it.

That story is a type for us: we too were all dead because we had become separated from the life of God, but when Jesus gets a hold of us, we come back to life. Like the staff, we blossom and produce fruit again. The secret of our life is the union we now have with God in Christ.

When God wanted to hallmark the man through whom He would speak to that generation, He used life as His evidence. God still does that today; He identifies who He is using by His life. In the times when council agencies and local government are wilting, we, the Church, should be blossoming and bearing fruit, ready to take on, with God-given resources, all the social care projects that they cannot any longer sustain.

The life of God today is the hallmark of who He is using! It's time for alignment; it's time for His Body, the Church to look like, sound like, and feel like the Head, Jesus. It's not the responsibility of the Head to change, but the Body! When people encounter you and your church, do they get a taste of Heaven or a taste of something else?

3

CREATED BY AND CREATED FOR

For by grace you have been saved through faith, and that not of yourselves; it is the gift of God, not of works, lest anyone should boast. For we are His workmanship, created in Christ Jesus for good works, which God prepared beforehand that we should walk in them (Ephesians 2:8-10).

Let's now take a moment to return to the message that the pioneers of the early Church carried. In this chapter, let's look at what was contained within that message that caused so many of the Pharisees to want to end the lives of those who carried it, especially Jesus and Paul. What was it about the message they carried that caused such a violent reaction from law lovers? That caused so many people to radically change and to find freedom beyond what they had dreamed? That motivated and mobilized an army to rise to its feet and make a difference across the face of the earth?

We know that the fundamental components of their message were love, grace, and faith—the good news of God's love openly displayed through what He sent Jesus to come and do for us. Have we understood the love of God as we should? Has it become the very measurement that determines who we are and what we will now do for Him? How about grace? Has our knowledge of the gift of grace fully saved us, or do we still strive by our own performance to get what we actually already own? And if we have understood grace and have entered into it by faith alone, are we now responding to it in a correct way? Join me as we take some time to answer these very fundamental questions, and a few more besides.

RETURNING TO THE MESSAGE OF GRACE

One of the fundamental things to grasp when returning to the blueprint for building His Church is to know the true essence of the message that the early Church carried: as a believer you have now been positioned and called. You have not just been positioned by God, you have also been called by Him to do good works. I pray that, as we unpack this foundational truth further, it will produce a fresh revelation within your life. When it comes to these incredible verses in Ephesians 2, the problem is often simply that many people stop reading too soon and miss the fullness of what Paul was teaching the Church. They often stop after verse 8 when they find out how He has wonderfully positioned them in grace, but I think verses 8, 9, and 10 working together help us to fully grasp what Paul was actually saying. When I read Ephesians 2:8-10, I see some things that are very profound and so important for every New Testament believer to understand. First, our standing as new creations is the sole product of His grace alone. We do not stand by self achievement, or by anything produced by our own performance or merit. We now stand positioned with confidence in a state of righteousness because of the success Jesus achieved by His death, burial, and resurrection. In the Father's sight, we are now in Christ, and His righteousness is fully ours. I am not speaking of self righteousness, but of an inherent righteousness that is the result of the success of the divine exchange He orchestrated on our behalf:

> *For He made Him who knew no sin to be sin for us, that we might become the righteousness of God in Him* (2 Corinthians 5:21).

This gift of perfect righteousness provides us with an infallible right-standing because it is not dependent upon our efforts to maintain it. Entrance into God's abundance of grace and this gift of righteousness are granted simply by taking a step of faith. Our positioning as heirs to the Father and joint heirs with the Son is the result of our belief in what He achieved on our behalf at the cross, and that alone (see Rom. 8:17). We now cease from our labors to produce a righteousness that pleases Him and instead enter into the rest that He has created for us (see Heb. 4:1-11). It's vital that we understand that we are saved (present tense) by His grace alone and that we enter into this all-saving grace in the same way that we enter into all the things God has for us...by faith. Indeed, just as Ephesians 2 declares with confidence and assurance, "by grace are we saved and that not of ourselves." It is a gift.

> *For if, by the trespass of the one man, death reigned through that one man, how much more will those who receive God's abundant provision of grace and of the gift of righteousness reign in life through the one man, Jesus Christ!* (Romans 5:17 NIV)

It is indeed this gift, given by God, which causes us to now rule and reign in life, knowing also that we can no longer boast in what we have done, but only in what Christ has done for us. As Paul said so well, "I have nothing to boast in but the cross of Christ" (see Gal. 6:14). Finally, the modern-day church is coming back to the place where preachers are no longer boasting in themselves and their own abilities, but are standing again in true humility, understanding that it's by grace alone. It's that amazing grace (undeserved, unmerited, and unearned favor) that we've all sung about for so many years. When we consider that classic hymn, we need to understand, and always remember, that there are two parts to that song representing a previous, and a current standing for the person who places faith in Christ. There's a wretch, and there's a man who's now saved! There's the blind man, and the man who now sees, and what divides those two very different experiences is the finished work of Jesus at Calvary. That alone qualifies the one who now stands truly righteous: "By grace you have been saved through faith" (Eph. 2:8).

As I stated before, when I read Ephesians 2:9-10, I see two components to this great revelation. Ephesians 2:9-10 reveals that I've been created by God, that I am now His workmanship, the product of what He achieved and created. However, verse 10 also tells me that "I've been created for good works," and this is the part I feel many Christians miss in their modern-day Christianity. They simply stop reading too soon. Yes, I've been created by God; I'm the product and workmanship of His grace, but the Bible doesn't stop there. Paul had not stopped speaking; he hadn't finished his sentence or fully made his point. With his next statement, he reveals that we have also been created for a purpose. This doesn't excite the lazy saint, but it certainly excites those who are hungry for God and hungry to be all He ordained them to be. There is a life He has destined for us to rule and reign in, but we will never rule and reign in life untill we know who we now are and what has now been entrusted to us. We must fully understand what He finished on the cross so that we know where we begin.

If you do not know where He finished,
you will never know where you begin!

Let us look at grace for a bit longer so that we can receive the fullness of the message Paul was bringing to the Church, a message that would empower and release the people of God to make a difference in the world and not to be left sitting, doing nothing, awaiting their collection. So that no one is confused concerning the first part of what Paul was revealing, let me say it again: we're saved by grace, we're saved by grace, we're saved by grace! What Jesus perfectly finished at the cross of Calvary brings us fully to our God-given new beginning as born-again new creations who have been forgiven, justified, and reconciled. We need to understand this. When we now read the Bible, it is vital for us to see the correct positioning of the cross of Christ within the overall truths that it shares.

Let me expand on this. As you know, within the Bible, there's an Old Covenant and there's a New Covenant. Using a more modern terminology, there's an old agreement between God and man for what obtained a state of righteousness, and there's a new agreement between God and man for what now obtains, maintains, and sustains a state of righteousness and justification in the life of the believer. Again, I love the wisdom of Paul when he says that we're to be diligent, unashamed workers who individually know how to rightly divide the Word of truth.

> *Be diligent to present yourself approved to God, a worker who does not need to be ashamed, rightly dividing the word of truth* (2 Timothy 2:15).

But what does it mean to divide the Word of truth? Where are we to cut or draw a dividing line in God's Holy Word, the Bible? I believe we are to place this dividing line in our Bibles at the point of the cross of Christ. At that moment, when Jesus died, was buried, and rose again, an old covenant ended, and a new one began. If we want to walk in successful Christianity, we need to be mature enough to know where all our self-effort to gain righteousness stops, and grace begins.

On the cross, Jesus declared to all of humanity, Heaven, and earth, "It is finished!" Those immortal words must now resound through the fiber of everything we once were, and indeed everything we now are. "It is finished." What did He mean by those words? Simply that the old agreement between God and man is finished because a new agreement is now in place established by His own blood, which fully paid for and removed our sins for all time.

Too many Christians are still mixing their covenants; they're living in a state of perpetual confusion trying to live out of corrupted theologies: "This side of the cross, God loves me, and it's all done—but let me just run again to the previous side of the cross and help Him out a little bit." God does not need your help, only your belief. If God needed your help, He would have asked for it. He doesn't need your ongoing help because what Christ did on the cross was a complete work. When Jesus said, "It is finished," He did not mean, "I'm finished." You now have a point by which you can rightly divide the Word of truth; you can know what applies to you and what no longer applies to you because of His perfect sacrifice.

Please understand; there's nothing evil or wrong about the Old Testament or about the law contained within it. The law was holy and based on how God lives. The problem wasn't with the law; the problem was with us and our ability to keep the law. The error was with humanity, not with the laws of God. The law was holy; the problem or breakdown was with us because we could never keep it.

Remember also that the divine purpose of the law was only ever to lead us to faith in Christ. Its purpose was to produce in us the realization that we could never keep God's righteous requirements in our own ability or strength. The law, like a tutor or escort, was purposed to lead us to faith in Christ, and when law had done its job and led us where it was meant to lead us, it was no longer needed (see Gal. 3:24-25). In the fullness of God's perfect timing, Christ came on our behalf and fulfilled the law perfectly in His flesh, paying the bill (debt) that was ours, and settling for the believer what the law demanded of us to gain the forgiveness, righteousness, and new life we needed, but never deserved. In paying the bill fully by His obedience, Jesus settled once and for all Adam's disobedience and released us from every curse, purchasing us back to Himself.

The Bible, throughout its pages, puts these truths in many ways. My personal favorite simply says it this way: "He who knew no sin [became] sin for us, that we might become the righteousness of God in Him" (2 Cor. 5:21). Again, too many people stop too soon when reading these words of Paul. They read about what Jesus became and did, but don't keep on reading about who we now are, "the righteousness of God in Him." The cross is the place of divine exchange. The cross is the place where an innocent Man approaches and takes on the guilt and shame of the world, but it's also a place where a guilty man or woman, a sinner such as I was, bound by sin with no hope, approaches the cross and leaves forgiven, righteous, and justified by God. The life, once guilty, is now forgiven and restored to a perfect innocence.

So, we rightly divide the Word of truth, not by drawing a line in it, but by placing a cross in it. A cross that is positioned at the end of the Old Testament, bringing us into the Book of Acts and into all the new things God has for us. The very sound of the covenant we have with God is now different. The language of the old agreement was "I do, I do, I do, I do, I do." The language of this new living agreement that was cut with the very blood of Jesus Christ is "it's done, it's done, it's done, it's done." Let those words resound in the very depths of who you now are in Christ. It's done! It's done! You can't pray to make yourself anymore saved; you can't read enough of the Bible to maintain your salvation. When we pray and read the Bible now, we do it because we want to and because we know what we already possess. It's now based on desire rather than obligation. You will never be more justified or righteous in the sight of God than you are now because your life is positioned in Him, by Him. What is His is now yours.

I would gladly continue to teach on His incredible grace and the righteousness it has produced for the remainder of this book, but grace is not the only point I'm trying to make in this chapter. However, before I move on, it is vital for me to check that we're all on the same platform of belief, or singing from the same hymn sheet, concerning how His grace has positioned us. We are now on the finished side of the cross. God hasn't commissioned us to live with one foot on each side of the cross, or to pop in and pop out of what He has already completed. That type of schizophrenic Christianity robs believers of their security and stability. Imagine if Paul had suffered from that type of Christianity. One moment he would be Paul, an apostle saved from who he once was; the next moment, he would slip into being Saul again, the old creation, and would kill everybody he once called friends. That would not have been good, would it? No. He knew who he no longer was, and he knew who God had made him o be by His grace. The truth is, you won't stop going to where you think is "home" until you realize it is not home to you anymore. Because you've been born again, your previous experience of who you are is no longer accurate. You've now been saved and repositioned by the finished perfect work of the cross—platform laid!

RESPONDING CORRECTLY TO THE MESSAGE OF GRACE

I now want to use the platform we have laid to look at our response to grace, or, to put it another way, "So what next?" As we have established, the Bible reveals that those who believe (place faith in Jesus) are completely saved by His grace. But what next? What do we do now? Do we just sit and await our collection? If there's nothing I can do to add to what He has done, what am I to do with the rest of my life? Do we just sit here and twiddle our thumbs till Jesus comes one day to pick us up? No. There are too many Christians doing that very thing because they misunderstand the proper response to God's grace. Grace should not produce a spiritual laziness in the Church; when taught correctly, it should produce a mobilized people who are doing things for God, motivated and fueled by desire, not by obligation or guilt trips. Let me say that again. There are too many Christians in the western church sitting on their blessed assurance doing nothing because they've misunderstood the correct response we are to have toward God's grace. Grace completes you and places you in right-standing with God, but, when you understand you've been saved and positioned by His grace, you should want to begin to do good works because you understand that you are the workmanship of God, created by Him for them.

For we are His workmanship, created in Christ Jesus for good works, which God prepared beforehand that we should walk in them (Ephesians 2:10).

I am not writing this to hand out guilt trips, but to tell you that if you're just wallowing in grace, inactive in your Christianity and local church, enjoying laziness divine, you have heard and understood only one verse of a more complete song. I want to sing the other verses of the same song to you to help you to understand the fullness of God's incredible plan that you have indeed been created by and created for.

HIS OLD AND HIS NEW WORKMANSHIP

We can compare ourselves in so many ways to the first created man, Adam, who was indeed God's first piece of human workmanship. He was created by God, born out of God's desire for fellowship and intimacy, born outside of his own effort to exist, simply made and positioned in accordance with God's intention and desire for him. Here are a few other comparisons we might make:

His first day was God's last day. God did everything He needed to when creating the world; then, finally, He made Adam and positioned him in the midst of His finished work. This is also what God did for us through the second Adam, Jesus, after Jesus had done all that was needed. We were made through new birth and, like Adam, were positioned in His completed work. So, our first day is also the result of His last day. Our first day is His Sabbath rest.

Adam was born a fully-formed adult and was born without a past. As new creations, we also are born "again" when we are adults, and as with him, we too have no past as it has been completely forgiven. It is as if it never happened.

The comparison I want to specifically look at right now is this one: Adam was God's workmanship. He was the produce of grace (God's doing, not his own intention or invention). He was what God had made outside of Adam's efforts or ability to help. Nevertheless, I don't believe for a minute that, after being created, Adam was left sitting in the garden making daisy chains or counting sheep. He would have found no fulfillment in that. Whatever God makes always has a purpose for its existence, and it always finds true fulfillment when living out its God-designed purpose.

Nowhere in Genesis does it say, "And God made Adam and positioned him comfortably, and he sat making daisy chains for the rest of his days." No. When you read Genesis, the great book of beginnings, you see that there was an "outflow" from his life. The outflow of his life was to maintain the Garden of Eden which belonged to God. This was not a chore; rather, it was a partnership because he was now in the family of God, and that garden was his garden, too. He wasn't God's Cinderella. God didn't say, "You know what? I need the grass cut. I'm gonna make Adam do it"; or, "I need the windows cleaned; I'll get Eve in on the picture here because I need some stuff done." No. There was an outflow to the life of Adam, and that outflow completed and fulfilled him. Notice in Genesis that God says to Adam, "I give you dominion" over this garden (Gen. 1:28). That garden represented God's Kingdom on the earth, His dwelling place, and possession. Not only did He give Adam dominion and authority to rule in and over the garden, He also gave him practical responsibility in the caretaking of it. He was in charge of both maintaining and advancing it. This, I imagine, would have involved a lot of real, practical, day-to-day stuff, like planting, growing, harvesting, and sorting out every part of this fruitful, vibrant garden. Again, let me say, he found fulfillment in this non-legalistic obligation.

Now stay with me. We're talking about Adam being both made and positioned for a purpose in that original garden. It is crucial to recognize that we, like Adam, have come into existence through nothing we've done. So we, like him, are God's workmanship. That's point one. We've also been created by God and find our origins in Him. But Ephesians 2:10 goes on to say, "And we are God's workmanship, created in [through] Christ Jesus, for good works." So, to me, proper

Christianity is to get people positioned in who they are by God's doing, but then also to get them functioning in these things that Paul calls "good works."

MADE FOR GOOD WORKS NOT DEAD ONES

So what are good works? Well, to start with, good works are not dead works. The Bible says, we're to *repent* from dead works (see Heb. 6:1; 9:14), but we're to *do* good works. So what's the difference between good works and dead works? Dead works are simply pointless endeavors, activities that produce nothing. For example, if you spend the whole morning trying to put the plug in the bath when the plug is already in the bath, or if you're bald and you spend all afternoon trying to shave your head, you're trying to do something that's already done. It's a pointless work or endeavor. Another pointless work is to try to daily save yourself when you're already saved. It's a dead work. It's pointless. It produces nothing, and it wastes time and energy.

So we're not talking about dead works because we're not Jehovah's Witnesses, we are Christians. Think about that. Jehovah's Witnesses have a whole lot of "doing" going on continually, knocking on doors, filling out charts, etc., but the sad reality is that the motivation for doing is to gain something from God. The reason they so often put us to shame with their passion for evangelism, the reason they relentlessly knock on so many doors and fill out so many charts is because everything that they're hoping for from God is dependent on it. It's all totally driven by their performance. It is driven by the slightest hope that they might get a glimpse of being a part of a small select bunch who get the chance to one day, maybe, go to Heaven. So they do to get; then they do to get again. Their motivation is to gain something that they don't presently have.

What about us who now live on the finished side of the cross, the side where it has all been done for us? When it comes to evangelism and making Jesus known, we should also do, do, do, but our motivation is very different. We do out of a revelation of what has already been done for us and what has already been given to us. We should not be doing to gain anything but because we've understood what's already been given to us by God. Notice the difference in motivation. They do to get; we should do because we have. We who know and have experienced the grace of God should, I believe, actually be more productive in what we do for God, knowing we come from a position of arrival and ownership.

If you study the words *good works* (in the Greek, *ergon*), you will see that they mean "business, employment, that which a person's occupied with, that with which a person undertakes to do, an enterprise, an act, a deed, things done or accomplished by the hand of a person."[1] In essence, *good works* simply means this: we've been created to do business, and not just any business, but *God's* business. "Well, that's a great message for the leaders, brother." Well, I am not talking just to the leaders; I'm talking to the Church, "the saints." You have been positioned by God's grace to do "God's business" on the earth, just like the first Adam.

When we grasp this reality, we then need to think about this matter even further. So, what is God's business? When we talk about doing God's business, I am reminded of that moment when Mary and Joseph were on their way back from the Passover feast and lost Jesus (see Luke 2:41). They lost Him for about three or four days. How serious is that! It's not like losing your car keys, or your wallet. They lost Heaven's master plan of redemption for all humanity who had been entrusted into their care. They eventually found Jesus in the temple (God's house) reasoning with the teachers concerning Scripture. When they asked where He had been, He responded, "Why did you seek Me? Did you not know that I must be about My Father's business?" (Luke 2:49). Remember, Joseph was only His stepfather. His real Dad was God; He had now come of age and knew He had to be about His real Father's business. We're all called—not just the leadership, but the whole Church—to be about God's business on the earth. Adam's dominion and responsibility was the natural Garden of Eden. For us, the

Church is the Garden of God, and the unsaved hurting world is where His Garden ever needs to be advancing into and taking over. Again, the responsibility for this advancement is not just with the leadership of the Church, it's with the whole Church, the Body of Christ. It's time to mobilize God's army! So when I think about what these good works are, I instantly think of two very basic, simple categories:

- The things that Jesus did.
- The things that are close to the heart of God.

What Jesus did as He was about the Father's business should be what we, His Church, are still busy with today. Jesus said of Himself, "For this purpose the Son of God was manifested [brought into the world], that He might destroy the works of the devil" (1 John 3:8). So, one of our mandates for good works is that we now live to destroy everything the devil builds. We are to destroy his works. When you study that word used for "the works of the devil," it is again the Greek word *ergon,* which means "business or enterprises." So, our business is to do God's business, which is to ruin the devil's business! Every time we see that the devil has spent years ruining a life, we take whatever time is needed to restore that life to everything that Christ died for it to be. That is definitely good works and time well spent. Like Jesus, we spend our time preaching the Gospel, healing the sick, and releasing those who are held captive, actually expecting to see, as He promised, greater things than He saw (see John 14:12).

And then there's the second category: loving what matters to God, loving what He loves. When I was studying this for me and my church, I suddenly realized how much God loves widows. Throughout the whole Bible, He mentions His love for widows and how He wants them to be taken care of. So, if God loves widows, we should love them too. I believe widows actually represents a broader category for us to think about, and that broader category would be all vulnerable people. It was not originally the job of the government to care for vulnerable people. That was, and will be again, the job or business of the Church of Jesus Christ. As local councils begin to lose finances for certain social care projects and give up on them, we need to rise up to bless, help, and stand by the vulnerable because the vulnerable and poor are always close to the heart of God. In the Old Testament, God says He's the Father to the fatherless. He's the Husband to the widow (see Ps. 68:5). Now, if that's what the Head and the heart wants to do, then the Body needs to carry those same desires also. These good works of God we are called to are not just preaching or teaching, they are also the social care and outreach projects that our churches need to provide for those in our community, and indeed the world. We are to be the Body of Christ, living out the desires of the heart of God, and being the physical hands and feet that go and do good things for others.

So how does what I'm teaching affect the Church? Simple, it should create in the believer a desire to do something for God, to be involved in good works that make a difference. Whether that's preaching, ministering, or all manner of social care projects, there should be a natural outflow from the life of every believer who understands that he or she is God's workmanship, created for good works!

Let me keep saying it till I am heard; this is not a call to the Ephesians 4 five-fold ministry leaders of the church. We will look at their role more closely in the next chapter. It is a call to the saints, the Church, every part and member of the Body, to get up and get active with the things that matter to God. It is a call for the Church to become missional minded in its thinking again, to be a people who do mighty exploits for God because they know their God (see Dan. 11:32).

As we will see in the next chapter, the primary purpose of your church leadership, according to Ephesians 4 (which is, in my opinion, still the relevant blueprint for church leadership), is not pastoral care. It is actually the equipping and mobilizing of the saints for "good works"—the things with which Jesus and the early Church busied themselves.

It's time for us to mobilize the Church. Remember what we said: the Church was never meant to be an event; it was meant to be the force of God upon the earth, doing His will, and turning communities upside-down. I believe it's now time to encourage the people who have misunderstood grace, who are seated comfortably in church, watching everyone else doing good works, to get out of their comfy chairs and be about the Father's business. And this should not be the product of legalistic obligation or guilt trips, but rather of a revelation that births a pure desire to care for what God cares for on the earth.

I honestly believe that the amount of needed pastoral care in the church would lessen if we did this. Let's face it, a high percentage of people who normally need, or feel they need, pastoral care, extensive counseling, and time, often just need to stop looking at themselves constantly and begin helping others. They need to look beyond their own needs, offenses, and wants in order to help other people. Please don't hear what I am not saying. I know that each church has a true percentage of genuine, needy people who need good pastoral support and ongoing care, but every church also has people who need to stop being so introspective, self-orientated, and self-obsessed. Their long-term help is actually to be found in making the decision to think about other people's needs instead. Some people just have far too much time to think about themselves and could do with spending some of that time on the good works to which God has called them. There is an old saying which says that the devil finds work for idle hands. I'd like to change that saying and put those hands to good works that will produce increase in God's Kingdom and in the lives of vulnerable, needy people.

Church leaders are there to equip the saints for good works. I'm a saint now, and so are you if you have been saved by Jesus. "Oh, here he goes…He's getting all self-righteous again." No, I'm Christ-righteous, because the Bible reveals that my life is now hidden in Christ; how much more righteous or saintly could I ever be than I am right now? And how would a few hundred years of death qualify me to be a saint if I'm not one now? It's time for the traditional Church to reform its thinking; Ephesians 4 speaks of *living saints,* people who are alive and who can be equipped to do and go now. A person does not get an angelic saucer over his or her head after being dead for a few hundred years. You are no more saintly in your future than you are right now in Him and seated with Him (see Eph. 2:6). So, here are a few questions I want to throw at you; then, I want to finish this chapter with an altar call for those who are not currently doing anything, a call in which you make some decisions about being mobilized. Perhaps your response involves going to a department head in your church and signing up to do things that will make your church the best it can be so that God's Kingdom can advance at a speed you've never imagined.

Mobilization is a key part of the success of the local church. It's good that people initially come and watch for a while, but they should not stay watching for too long. Like an escalator, they should be ever moving up in their commitment to and ownership of the needs and the mission of their church. At any given time, we should have three specific groups of people in our church: spectators, servants, and stewards. Unless they are transfer growth, most people start off as spectators and, like the season of dating in a natural relationship, this is not wrong. This is actually quite normal. People come and listen, are saved or re-connected, then continue to listen further to see if your church could be the right spiritual home for them. I believe that it is then normal for this to change, and abnormal when it does not.

After a while, the spectator should say, "OK, enough sitting and watching—let me now get involved with something that makes church happen." This is when they move up the escalator to being a servant. They get on a team and become a part of making the church or its various projects happen weekly. They should eventually want to be even more involved and take responsibility for a department or a team rather than just be on it. This is when they are no longer servants, but stewards in the house; they don't care only about what the church needs today, but they also have a heart for what it needs for its future. I believe this is normal behavior in the house of God, and leaders should encourage and propagate this very natural response in the hearts of those who come to church. In doing so, the church is blessed and equipped, but, believe me, so also are the people. They will get so much more out of church than if they were left to sit and watch. The Bible says that we are all servants and stewards of the mysteries of God: "Let a man so consider us, as servants of Christ and stewards of the mysteries of God" (1 Cor. 4:1).

I believe that the fashion within church life is changing. We have known a season where great emphasis has been put on well-run meetings and events, good-looking stages, and classy performances. None of these things are wrong if they come from a heart that wants to make church the best it can be for God and for people who need to connect with Him, but I feel that we are in a season shift when God is putting greater emphasis on this aspect of His blueprint for a healthy effective Church: the equipping, mobilizing, and sending of people to take care of His business.

Naturally speaking, fashion is such a funny thing. One season everyone wears the same thing, and then the fashion suddenly changes, and people react differently. Some people are ahead of fashion, others keep up with it, and others are always behind it. When it comes to what is happening spiritually in God's Church, we can see the same thing. I want to be ahead of the fashion. I don't want to be wearing what other people were wearing many years ago when things have obviously moved on. I want to get church fashion back to what is fashionable to God. To me, that is still the vision of the Church we find in the Book of Acts, where every member is a minister, and the people are taking active ownership for advancing the mission of the Church. Let's change what's currently fashionable if it's not current with His blueprint.

THE GARDEN NEEDS YOU

Just as Adam was placed in the Garden of Eden to manage and tend it, so you have been positioned in the Body of Christ to be a part of what it is doing now and what it is dreaming to do in the future. How could we not be committed to seeing God's 21st-century Garden, the Church, in our generation advance and take new ground? The reality is that every local church always has positions that need to be filled by committed people. Let's have a culture within our churches that inspires and equips people to take ownership for the needs of their church. When I think about natural gardening, even though I don't know much about gardening, I believe Adam would have had a varied and busy life. There were all manner of responsibilities that he would have had on a weekly basis, from sowing and harvesting to taking care of seedlings and young saplings. It's the same for the Garden of God today, which is the Church. Your church needs each member of it to get involved. It doesn't want people to feel obligated; rather, it wants them to run in saying, "I'm so saved by grace that I can't control myself. Just give me something to do, Pastor!" That's what I believe is a correct and normal response to God's grace.

Just as Adam worked with those seedlings and saplings, your children's church and kids' programs need workers who are not just passing through on their way to pulpit ministry or better opportunities. They need servants who will say, "If this is what You want me to do, God, for all of my days I will take good care of these seedlings and saplings so that they grow into little plants and become mighty oaks in Your house." The youth work needs workers, and the set-up teams and other practical teams need workers too. So many teams in our churches need people to step up and get involved! What about the midweek projects that the church runs? Or the programs that take care of unsaved people's practical needs? It's time for everyone who calls a church their church to get involved. May people in church now arise from any seated position they have unknowingly settled for and get busy doing God's business because, don't forget, God's people were not only created by, they were also created for!

A perfectly functioning church is like a perfectly functioning body. Within the body of an athlete who runs a race, each physical member knows its part and functions as that part within the body for a common cause; success is then continually produced and races are won. When some parts don't do anything or only intermittently do their part, other members have to take up the extra strain. Before long, the parts that are doing more than they should be, begin to be affected by the extra strain and can be weighed down, even damaged by it, lessening the overall potential of the body of that athlete.

The Body of Christ should never be like this. We should see every person (part) discovering and being committed to being the best part they can be within the functioning body of the local church. As Ephesians 2:10 says, every member should be finding fulfillment and taking responsibility for that "which God prepared in advance for them to do." The bottom line is, if you are not doing what was prepared in advance for you to do, then someone else must do it for you. That places undue weight on others and lessens the overall effectiveness of the Body.

For every minister reading this, I hope it inspires you to make a fresh commitment to equipping and mobilizing your church to do good works. To the broader Church who is reading this, to the faithful, I say, keep on serving and giving yourself away. God is so worth it. And to those who have been seated in grace but never knew it, it's time to get up and begin to do, not just be. The Kingdom, more specifically, your church needs you. Next, we will look at being a people who are not just *doing* for God, but *going* for God too.

ENDNOTE

1. "Ergon"; see http://concordances.org/greek/2041.htm.

4

RETURNING TO THE GREAT COMMISSION

Later He appeared to the eleven as they sat at the table; and He rebuked their unbelief and hardness of heart, because they did not believe those who had seen Him after He had risen. And He said to them, "Go into all the world and preach the gospel to every creature. He who believes and is baptized will be saved; but he who does not believe will be condemned. And these signs will follow those who believe: In My name they will cast out demons; they will speak with new tongues; they will take up serpents; and if they drink anything deadly, it will by no means hurt them; they will lay hands on the sick, and they will recover" (Mark 16:14-18).

As we consider further the ancient lines of that first blueprint for the Church as laid out by Jesus, we almost immediately notice the passionate emphasis that He places on the "great commission" and being a missional-minded people. Before we go any further, I would like to define two important terms that I will be using in this book: *missional* and *attractional.* To be *attractional* is to put a lot of effort into making stage, performance, and church experience first-class. It is not about being seeker friendly, referring to keeping away from certain subjects and spiritual issues to be more palatable; rather, it puts emphasis on how things look and feel, sometimes at the cost of content. To be *missional* is to think about *going;* it is outward looking rather than introspective and bound by church walls. A missional-minded people have their hearts set on going and doing rather than staying and watching; they have resolved in their hearts to be a bunch of goers, daily allowing their lives to be the vehicle that Jesus can use to go where He is desiring next—whether that be local, national, or beyond. Will you be someone who carries Jesus in your everyday life?

In this chapter, we want to look again at the call of the great commission to the Church, and to consider if being attractional and gathering a crowd is what Jesus actually wanted. We will ask some provocative questions concerning who is in the crowd and what the crowd is actually achieving for God. We will take time to look again at our mandate to go, and also find out where we are meant to be going as we dare to stand and join the generations who have gone before us, to fulfill this great commission given us by the Head of the Church, Jesus Christ.

SO WE HAVE A CROWD...

This journey of rediscovery started for me one Sunday morning when I sat and looked at the good crowd of people that my team and I had successfully attracted over 14 years of faithfully ministering to our city and surrounding areas. We had drawn them in part by our commitment to being an "attractional type" church, putting on great events and providing great service. We had certainly gathered a pretty big crowd through our multi-congregational way of doing church. But this particular morning, as I looked at them, my heart was asking some questions I had not asked for quite a while. It was an unusual Sunday for us because we had held our morning service in a large theater in the city in order to see if it could be a possible future venue for us, as we had again outgrown our current one. Because of good growth, we had gone to two services and were now looking for a new location for the main Sunday morning service.

The venue we had hired presented a few more difficulties than our regular one, especially when it came to parking and a sufficient number of smaller rooms for our kids' programs. The school we had formerly used had been perfect in both of these areas, but the size of the crowd that was now coming every Sunday meant we had to look for a new home. What I noticed this particular morning was that these inconveniences produced a number of different responses from the people who called Family Church home. For those with a "can do" spirit, it was the opportunity to overcome some obstacles and challenges. For others, even though it was indeed more inconvenient, it made perfect sense to "try the building on" this particular weekend in order to see if it was a viable option. These people gladly put up with the inconveniences that morning.

Then, I could not help but notice some gaps as I looked out into the crowd. These gaps were obviously created by the ones who were not there. Some had genuine reasons for not being there, but others thought it a good week to "have off"; these individuals had clearly weighed the purpose of the "trying it out" against the inconvenience of it and were staying away until things moved "back to normal." We had a great service that morning but soon realized that the theater venue would not work for us long-term, as we could not do the kids' work or take care of other responsibilities due to the lack of smaller rooms. So even though it was a fun morning, our pursuit for a perfect venue would have to continue.

As I said, this morning my heart was beating differently as I heard certain sounds coming from within some of "our crowd." I heard the sound of settlers rather than pioneers, the sound of a crowd that was used to having things put on and made easy or convenient for them. My question was no longer, "Do they want to come to our church?"

I was now asking myself, and some of my leaders, "Is this the type of church we want?" "Is this the type of church I want to spend the currency of my days leading?" I was not upset in any way, but some serious questions came through my mind that morning; and in my message, I voiced a number of them to the church. I asked the church some very straight questions concerning who and what was in the crowd that we had gathered, not to make anyone feel guilty, but to see if we were all on the same hymn sheet when it came to building Church. I wanted to see if we were just a bunch of consumers content to sit, or if we were indeed the consumed, the stirred—a people wanting to do something radical for God in our generation.

That morning, I spoke on crowds, and looked at some of the different types of crowds that called our city home. I then compared our church crowd to each of them, concerning their objectives and their passion. First, I looked at the "theater crowd," those people who would normally come to the venue we were trying on that morning, but who are naturally a consumer-minded crowd. When they come, they come to watch a show, they come to be taken care of and entertained. They pay to watch the entertainment being provided, and there's nothing wrong with that—very little participation is ever expected of a theater crowd. "But what about the Church?" I asked. "Is that how it is meant to be for us? Are we called to just attract people? To get them saved and then let them sit there and be spiritually entertained while a smaller crowd of faithful servants give their lives away week in and week out to make Church the best it can be?" No, my heart could no longer find any satisfaction, or passion, in developing or leading a church that had this as its unseen objective or agenda. God's people have been called to be so much more than that.

The next crowd that I spoke about was one that every city has— the "soccer crowd." This crowd is made up of spectators of all ages and both genders. This crowd, in my opinion, displays a passion that is often inspirational. Like the theater crowd, this crowd is also about entertainment, but it's not the same. Yes, these people are there to watch, but at a much higher level, with a much higher buy-in. These people are there to support.

Our soccer ground in Portsmouth is an old one and is unusually positioned in the center of our city where there is nowhere near enough parking for even a quarter of those who regularly come to watch a match. Previously, because I was somewhat intrigued by this crowd, I spent time studying the culture of the soccer ground and its supporters, watching the faithful commitment of those who called the team, their team. Growing up in the city, I had often noticed that, whenever a match was on, the supporters would have to park not just ten streets away, but more often 20 or more streets away. Every time the team played, some would walk 30 or 40 minutes to get to the ground because of the severe lack of parking in our city. As you watch the "Blue Army" walk through the streets on match day, they are unstoppable. Rain or shine, they never moan or groan, but joyfully, expectantly walk with a fast, determined stride to get to their club, to watch their team play, and to give them the support they need to win. Yes, they would like better parking or a new ground with an underground parking lot with elevators, but it does not matter that much to them. What matters is to get there on time for the game so they can be the supporters they claim to be. They rarely moan about financially supporting the team, paying for tickets, or purchasing season tickets to be a part of each game. They never mind lining up to get into the stadium or ground—it is to be expected because of the volume of people. Never is there any intention to stay away because there might be "too many coming"; in fact, the thought of a full stadium because of a big game only means that they come in larger droves, willing to park and walk even further than before. Why? Because this is their team!

What about when the team is "playing away"? Like worker ants, they organize pick-up points where they will meet, making sure they leave on time to be at the away game when needed. And then there is the ambiance: every time a goal goes in, they all in unison stand up and cheer. When there is a foul against their team, each and every one of them has a verbal response to share. I love watching seemingly nice old men turn into bleacher lunatics with uncompromising points of view when the visiting team does something that is "just not right." I must admit that when I go to a soccer match, being a person who loves to study human behavior, I get much more fun out of watching fans respond to the game than I do from the game itself. I love the passionate responses of everyday people who are immersed in the game to such a degree that, without noticing, they forget their low self-esteem and lack of confidence and join in with what is happening on the field with every fiber of their being, believing and standing with every other supporter present for the success of their team.

I shared on the "soccer crowd" to my crowd that was seated listening to me that morning. Don't get me wrong, this crowd had a large percent of committed people who were more sold-out than soccer fans. But I had to say to them, "Let's be honest, we cannot say that, as a group, we match the passion of the soccer crowd. It's not that we can't in the future, but we don't right now. For now, we need to focus on catching up with them, not on overtaking them."

Let's ask the questions we need to. How many in the church, especially those who have enjoyed our offer to come and sit comfortably, would even consider walking two streets to get to where the church was "playing next"? How many would not be put off by the rain or lines of people? Certainly, such people were with us now in the church crowd, but not in the number I now wanted, or that we would need in order to change the city. We needed a shift that would cause more of the comfortably seated saints to arise, stand, and serve with those who faithfully lived to make it happen each week. This shift could cause us to get where we wanted to go a lot faster—and it would be created, not through a sense of obligation, but through an increase in love. How much do they love God and His house? I once heard it put it this way: "The measure of your love will always determine the length of your journey." I think that statement packages the reality of what we are actually dealing with very well. It's not about more servitude or greater commitment from church people. It's much simpler than that. It's about how much we love God because, in every other area of our lives, this principle remains true. What we are willing to do, or how far we are willing to go—even what we are willing to put up with—is directly related to the love we have for something or someone.

The soccer crowd inspired me by giving me a benchmark, or a visual goal, for how God's crowd, the Church, should look and behave. It's just a matter of understanding our purpose as God's crowd. The fans at the soccer field do all that they do, including cheering their heads off, for a ball of air being kicked into a goal. How much more passion and commitment should we display when we understand that our win is not a ball in a net, but a soul saved from hell? Oh, how we should cheer, stand, and jump every time a soul is saved in one of our meetings! Alternatively, we can sit and smile politely, unaware of what just spiritually transpired in the life of that person. Like the thief on the cross, a soul just passed from death to life and became Heaven bound. I know which response I would prefer; how about you?

I also firmly believe the sound of our praise and worship should exceed the sound of theirs. What comes from the Church every time we meet should always proportionally be louder than what comes from the local soccer field. They are singing the praise of natural men who shine for a mere moment; we shout the fame of the Alpha and Omega, who saved a dead humanity, redeeming them perfectly from their sins, qualifying them to enjoy all that God has for them. Please don't think me a killjoy; I believe it is good to have other interests that make you cheer—but surely our greatest, most passionate cheer should belong to the One who saved, not a leather ball, but rather our lives, our souls, our all. I must admit it does annoy me when I see believers passionate outside the church for sports and other activities, yet when they get into church, they become nonresponsive and passionless toward all God is and does. It's time to turn that around and to get the loudest shout in the city back into the camp of the Lord.

Whatever was happening in me began to get worse, and over the next few weeks, I continued to ask real questions—not of the church, but of myself. Fundamental questions like, "What is the Church? Why are we here? What does God want us to do in this generation?" It was like God had put itching powder down my back, and I had questions that needed to be scratched until I reached satisfactory conclusions. I knew that I was in the process of developing some new persuasions concerning the next leg of our church journey. Over the next weeks and months, I scratched, I thought, I looked for what really mattered. Was it just about being attractional, drawing people, getting them saved, and positioning them in church safely with Heaven-bound lives? Or was there more? Was I severely missing something? Why was I bored when the church looked so healthy and seemed to be doing so well? I scratched and I scratched, and it was all good because I began to hear God's heart again concerning what He wanted. It was not that we had been out in left field in either our values or our practice, but that we were not passionate about the things He was passionate about. We needed to stop, rediscover, and return to the original blueprint; that blueprint would produce a church that could make a difference in the city, the nation, and even the world. That church would be on its feet, ready to go—not seated and waiting for the next piece of spiritual entertainment we would provide. It was time to GO.

A RETURN TO BEING MISSIONAL MINDED

In the midst of all this scratching came a fresh revelation. As I considered the desires of Jesus and what the early Church had dedicated itself to, I saw again the importance of the great commission, and the passion and purpose that Jesus had when He told the Church to *go*. He commissioned them to be a people who go and make the difference. That, I believe, was the very DNA of the early Church. They were not insular or inward looking; they had hearts set on going. In all they did, they were mission minded. They never let momentary inconvenience or discomfort stop them from going. They never let the relationships they had formed or the preferences they individually had keep them from going; they saw the need beyond the walls of their own existence and just kept on going.

I then realized that this was actually a very large part of what was causing my internal discomfort. I had worked hard to get as many people in one place as I could, all with good intentions to see them saved and prepared for Heaven, but I had not put enough emphasis on equipping, training, and sending. This was one of the reasons we had stagnated and why a large percentage was just "happy to be seated." Now, I could see it and was ready to bring some radical change to this area of the culture and heart of our church. I was no longer going to make people feel so welcomed, and well seated, that they did nothing. Instead, we would remain attractional to get them in. We would continue putting on excellent, well-run meetings, because God is worth the best we can do, but that would no longer be our sole purpose. From this day, we would put a greater emphasis on equipping, empowering, and releasing God's people to do the works of the ministry. We would remain attractional to draw people, but we would now have a strong underlying missional agenda for everything we did. I was standing over His blueprint again, the great commission enthusing me with a fresh passion, and it felt uncontainable. It was like I had awoken from a sleep. I realized afresh that the Church was not just an event, it was a force, His army, on the face of the earth positioned to fulfill the desires of God. I felt so strongly that God was giving me a word for His Church in this generation, and that word was simply this: "The King wants to mobilize His Army." All I knew was that my boredom was well and truly gone, fresh vision rushed through my veins, and the excitement I had unknowingly lost had now returned.

I had spent 14 years trying to fill the church, but now I wanted to spend my time trying to empty it, not driving people away with offensive preaching but rather mobilizing, equipping, and sending people to make a difference in their worlds.

I now began to deliver my thoughts and conclusions to the church, speaking of how we would, from this point in our journey, be missional minded in our outworking. Church would now be a place where greater emphasis would be put on equipping people to do something for God. If they were determined to just sit and watch, they were always welcome, but my preaching, I warned them, from this point on might annoy and irritate them. I was not trying to get people to sit comfortable anymore, but to get up and get moving in what God had for them to do. Together, we would now be aiming at the target of "every member a minister." Imagine the ramifications as that reality is lived out in our churches and communities! Imagine what we could do and how fast we could do it when that dream, or target, becomes a living reality in the churches we attend. To my delight, these thoughts were welcomed with great excitement; in fact, the church was so ready for this, it was like the match was hitting the strike paper of a matchbox with perfect timing. I think that, like me, many of them were also a bit bored, wondering if our meetings, well-decorated stages, and well-run programs were really the totality of what God had destined us for.

Instantly, we made plans to plant more congregations, train and equip people, and send them out. We would purposefully create a void in the church again so God could fill it; we would create spaces in the leadership and departments of the church so people could step up into duties they had never done before and grow. It was only a matter of weeks before church felt dangerous again; indeed, it felt like a force and no longer just a well-run event. In communicating these new thoughts and persuasions with the church, I was quite firm in my persuasion but took time to show them God's blueprint and design in it all. For example, I reintroduced them to Ephesians 4 and the God-given role of their church leadership.

EPHESIANS 4 LEADERSHIP

And He Himself gave some to be apostles, some prophets, some evangelists, and some pastors and teachers, for the equipping of the saints for the work of ministry, for the edifying of the body of Christ, till we all come to the unity of the faith and of the

*knowledge of the Son of God, to a perfect man, to the measure
of the stature of the fullness of Christ* (Ephesians 4:11-13).

Notice this passage says, "He gave." These people (apostles, prophets, evangelists, pastors, and teachers) are given by God for a purpose; they are not the design of man. They are the desired gifts of God given for the health and well-being of His Body. Notice that this passage does not say that their primary purpose is to pastorally care for the church (though there should be good pastoral care in the church). It says that their primary role is to "equip the saints for the work of the ministry." The fivefold ministry gifts help the saints become active in all that they have been destined by God to be. The primary role of any New Testament church leader is to equip the saints; are we doing that? Are we equipping saints, or are we just seating, storing, and entertaining them? Are we—with all our well-run meetings and programs—training, equipping, and releasing people to do the things (good works) that God has for them to do?

These, I believe, are the questions we need to be asking in today's church; and if we find ourselves wanting, we need to do something about it. There is a big job to be done. The King wants to mobilize His Army, and the mobilized saints remain God's master plan for getting that job done. The Greek word for "works of ministry" in Ephesians 4 is *ergon;* that same word was used in Ephesians 2 to describe the believer, who is created for "good works." Among other things, *ergon* means "business, endeavors, enterprises and the work of a person's hand." So holding it in context again, Ephesians 4 teaches us that church leadership has been positioned by God to equip the saints, "God's crowd," to "do God's business on the earth."

Imagine what would happen, and the effect we would have on our cities, if we dared to turn the pyramid of who is involved and active in the church around? Traditionally, we have been handed a pyramid that has the leader at the top, then his team, and on down the hierarchy of active involvement till we reach the crowd at the bottom, who mostly watches a small number of leaders do nearly everything. What small potential, or fist of impact, there is with that type of pyramid. Now see what happens when we turn that pyramid or way of operating around, not in the context of who is in charge of leading the church, but in reference to who does what on a weekly basis and the involvement that comes from the crowd concerning the common commission each church has been given. What if we turned it around so that the leader is now at the bottom, empowering the saints with his or her leadership team to do God's business? You can see on the diagram below how the punch or potential of the church increases in an incredible way with this simple shift of thinking. The lower pyramid is, I believe, how the pyramid of involvement looked in the early church, and how it needs to look today in our churches if we want to match their impact in our generation.

It's time to equip and release the saints to do God's business: leading people to Christ in their daily worlds, praying for the sick, casting out devils, and setting the captives free. We need a mobilized army who will go off each week in different directions driven by their different passions and abilities—some equipped to meet the needs of the community through social care; others released to minister into the various subcultures of our communities (for example, youth, the elderly, and children). There are so many platforms for so many saints to take their place upon, but it starts with heartbeat and desire. It's not good enough for the leaders to have the desire to equip the saints. The saints must want to be equipped; otherwise, it turns into another exercise of legalism and obligation-based works. I pray that the saints begin to arise and put a demand upon the leadership to equip and train them. That is a problem I believe every church leader would welcome with open arms—people who formerly sat and watched now wanting to be equipped and sent! Jesus wants to mobilize His Army; how does that affect *you?*

THE DAY OF THE DONKEY

"Go into the village opposite you, where as you enter you will find a colt tied, on which no one has ever sat. Loose it and bring it here. And if anyone asks you, 'Why are you loosing it?' thus you shall say to him, 'Because the Lord has need of it.'" So those who were sent went their way and found it just as He had said to them. But as they were loosing the colt, the owners of it said to them, "Why are you loosing the colt?" And they said, "The Lord has need of him" (Luke 19:30-34).

I love this account of the disciples going to collect a donkey for Jesus. The disciples were told to go into a village and collect a donkey, which belonged to someone else, for Jesus. We see the owners suddenly appear when the disciples are helping themselves to their property. When the disciples are asked, "What are you doing?" They respond with, *"The Lord has need of him."* Hearing this, the owners let them take the donkey and waved them on their way. Perhaps they felt the authority of the Lord in the disciples' response. Or, perhaps this was a prearranged deal between Jesus and the owners. Perhaps they had experienced Jesus change their lives in one way or another and said, "Look, we don't have much; we have a donkey if ever You need it—just let us know." Jesus now needed a vehicle to go somewhere, remembered the kind offer, and simply cashed in what had been committed for His use.

What I really want you to notice, however, is the type of vehicle Jesus chose to enter the most significant city of its time, Jerusalem. It was not a golden chariot nor a fine black stallion, but a very simple, everyday donkey. It was the back of this often overlooked, common creature that was chosen to carry the greatest package ever carried, humanity's hope: Jesus. When you study the word *donkey*, one translation says, "beast of burden." How fitting that this "beast of burden" would get to carry the One who would, in turn, carry the sins and burdens of the whole world. Why did Jesus not choose a golden chariot or a stallion? Maybe because He never came as the Pharisees had expected Him to, as a saving messiah riding into town on a golden chariot, but rather as His Father in Heaven wanted Him to, a servant King born in a manger, walking through everyday people's worlds with meekness and authority.

Also, He didn't choose a stallion because stallions can have big egos, and He did not need an ego to carry Him on this very important journey. Maybe, when the applause and shouts began at the gate of Jerusalem, a stallion would have thought the applause was all about him and would have reared up in pride causing the rider, that very important package, to be thrown off. No. This moment of entry into Jerusalem was all about the rider, Jesus, and the vehicle He chose was perfect because it spoke of His humility, meekness, and servant heart. Let's face it, donkeys are not known for their fine looks; they *are* known for their faithfulness and steadfastness. When you want a package to leave one place on time and arrive safely at another, you can rely on a donkey. Today, Jesus still wants to go places and is looking for someone to give Him a lift. He wants to go into your cities, colleges, and neighborhoods, and He is looking for a vehicle that will be faithful. How about you? Will you bear your back, your life, to carry Him? Will you be a donkey He can use? I believe that the day of the superstar and the stallion is over. It's the day of the donkey. He is looking for a ride. Will you carry Him?

Jesus said to His disciples when He commissioned them to go bring Him the donkey, "Loose it and bring it to Me." The story records that the disciples found the donkey tied up, just as Jesus had said and, indeed, loosed it and brought it to Him. That day, everything changed for that donkey—probably, all it had known up to that day was walking around in never-ending circles tied to a pole, stopping every now and then to eat hay and look at a world that it could not enter because of its captivity. Here's a thought: Jesus didn't want to loose the donkey simply because He liked donkeys and wanted it to enjoy its freedom or take it to a donkey sanctuary—He loosed it for a purpose. It was given its freedom so that it could carry the presence of God, Jesus, where He needed to go. Wow! What a day that was for that donkey to go from being bound to a pole, to being a carrier of a move of God—Jesus. You have probably worked out my comparison, right? Each of us is like that donkey. We were tied up to sin, bound and not free; then Jesus sent His message of freedom and liberated us from the captivity we knew. What wonderful news! But it is not just about your freedom. It's great that you're set free, but what now? Jesus wants to ride upon your life, as He did that liberated donkey, to bring His message of freedom and spirit of life to the other places where it is so needed. He has a purpose for you.

I don't know about you, but I don't want to be a free donkey, running around a field doing my own thing. I am so grateful for the freedom He has given me, grateful enough to offer that freedom back to Him for His plans and intentions. How about you? It was for freedom that Christ has set you free, but that freedom also has a Kingdom transporting purpose to it. Will you be free, or freed and brought to Him for His purposes?

One final point that I noticed when I read this same account in Matthew 21:1-3, is that Jesus sent the disciples to loose and bring to Him a donkey, and her young colt also. When I thought about this, I understood that God is not just looking at releasing faithful carriers for this generation through us, but He is also passionate about the next one. I believe true success is when we allow Him to loose our lives and use them for His Kingdom purposes, but, also, that we bring the next generation to Him, taking the time to raise them up to love and serve Him as we have decided to do. The next generation, our colts, need to see us carry and serve the Lord. We will inspire them to do the same in their generation. We then raise an army to follow in our tracks. Jesus wants us and them. It's our responsibility to let the children and young people in our world find Jesus and His purposes while they are young, raising them up in the way they will go. So, when they get old, they won't depart from those ways (see Prov. 22:6). We should protect them from all the religious cobwebs we had to beat our way through to find Him, indeed carrying them on our shoulders so they can see further than we have. Whether you are a parent, grandparent, or a children's or youth worker, remember, and be inspired today, that your influence over the colts in your world is powerful. Make sure that you are influencing them toward Jesus, just as you are running after Him for yourself. We are God's master plan for this moment; they are His master plan for the moments that are to follow ours.

THREE SPHERES OF INFLUENCE

But you will receive power when the Holy Spirit comes on you; and you will be My witnesses in Jerusalem, and in all Judea and Samaria, and to the ends of the earth (Acts 1:8 NIV).

The Church still has this great commission to "Go," and if we take our coordinates from the above verse, we see we are called to go to three different places, or spheres of influence. The Church needs to be training and releasing people to be effective go-ers and to have godly influence and impact in all three of them.

Acts 1:8 mentions three specific locations. Like the ripple effect that is produced when a rock hits a pond, so the impact of what God has done in us should affect the surrounding spheres of influence in our lives. The early Church was instructed by Jesus to go and have influence for Him in Jerusalem, Judea, and Samaria and to the ends of the earth. This was indeed a huge commission for them to give their lives to see fulfilled. Within these three locations, we can see the three mission calls that every church should be involved in on a day-to-day basis. So what do they represent to the local church and indeed every individual believer?

GOING IS A NEW MINDSET!

Missional thinking is always made up of three common components. These are praying, giving, and going; at different times any one, or any combination of these three, are needed from us. Sometimes we need to be praying; other times we need to give—maybe so that someone else can go—but there are times when we need to be ready and equipped to go as well. When I speak of these three spheres of influence, I want you to apply them to two realities the local church you lead or are a part of and also your individual life; the great commission is not just a corporate experience or commission, but also an individual one. As we speak of these three ripple effects, think about your local, national, and worldwide impact.

YOUR JERUSALEM

Jerusalem, I believe, represents your local sphere of influence—the city, town, or village you live in—as well as your local everyday life, the places you work or where you attend school. The circles of influence you have are made up of your neighborhoods, communities, and the family and friendship circles that are unique to each of us. God wants your life and your church to have an impact here first. When you speak about missions, or being missional minded, people straight away think about jumping on a plane and going to the ends of the earth, but actually, God says that we need to focus on our local world, our Jerusalems, first. I actually think it is easier to go and do missions somewhere else in the world because no one knows you; you can pretend to be whoever you want to be for a couple of weeks since no one knows you as anything different. But in your local world, that is not the case. That's why it is sometimes more challenging. You need the empowerment of God to be a witness in your Jerusalem more than you do at the ends of the earth— to leave your house in the morning as a "go-er" for God with a mission-minded heart that says, "God, I am going to live for You today in a way that turns the heads of those who know me toward You."

The great commission says go into the world, but I believe that always starts with believers going into their world, the world that is unique to them. We need to understand that every time we leave our house in the morning, we actually enter God's mission field for us, not just when we get on a plane, and are called to be His witnesses at home. The reality is, you don't have to go far to be a missionary-minded person. It starts with a change of mindset that brings the change to your whole world. This change of mindset is simply, "It's time to live beyond myself, to live beyond the shoreline of my own existence." When you purpose to live beyond yourself, you have actually started the journey of a missionary. What do I mean by "live beyond yourself"? Dare to live beyond your comfort, preference, likes, and such things. Live for what benefits and helps others, even when it is to your cost. This is the very essence of mission-minded thought, and it's this essence, or heartbeat, that we live out in all three of the spheres we are called to, but it must start in our Jerusalem, our present world, and, indeed, within our local church.

Let me be so bold as to say our churches would be so much more effective if more of the people who called them home purposed to "live beyond themselves." It is amazing how our self-ordained rights and preferences keep us from functioning in the house in a way that could so accelerate its impact and potential.

Certain teams in the church always need more people to be on team. Those are the departments that don't seem too glamorous, but are actually backbone ministries to each and every local church, like hosting teams, children's church, and nursery to name just a few. It's so frustrating for church leaders to constantly make appeals for help in these areas. Leaders who make such appeals usually see people look at them in a way that says, "Excuse me, that is not what I want"; "That does not suit me"; "That would be an inconvenience to my Sunday." Herein lies the fundamental problem. It's time to live beyond those attitudes for the advancement of Jesus' church in our communities.

This non-missional, preference-orientated type of Christianity can manifest in many different ways, but we must remind ourselves that it's not all about us or what we like, but about those who don't yet know Him. I have had people come to me after services, people who have been saved many years but who have not actually done too much, and say things like, "We liked three of the songs this morning, but we really did not like that last one," or "We're not sure if the lights are what we like." I used to be more polite with my response, whereas, I am not so polite these days and usually respond by saying, "Maybe today, all we did was not about you and what you prefer. Maybe it was about the four people who responded to Jesus for the first time." Maybe church is not all about us, or our preferences; rather, it is a common team effort to win for God that which God wants—people saved and discipled!

If we are the Body of Christ, then we need to carry the same heartbeat that He carries. Let us remind ourselves that His heartbeat beats for things beyond our individual lives and personal preferences. His heartbeat is for lost people to be saved. He still loves to go after the one; He puts value on the one who is not yet in the flock. We only have to read Luke 15 to rediscover that heartbeat.

Living beyond the boundaries of our own lives and preferences does not happen when we go on a mission trip to the other side of the world, but when we leave our homes in the morning and function weekly in our local churches. May I challenge you, concerning your personal Jerusalem, to do something for someone else that you would have preferred not to do. Do something to help your church that requires you to leave your personal comfort zone. If you do this, you will be surprised at what God starts to do in, and through, your life. The great commission calls for us to "get over ourselves," to "live beyond ourselves," and to prefer others.

> *Be kindly affectionate to one another with brotherly love, in honor giving preference to one another* (Romans 12:10).

The very first journey we must take if we want to be missionaries for God is the journey beyond the boundaries of ourselves, including our personal comfort and preference, for the benefit of others. The fact is that, until we live beyond ourselves, we are not missionaries anywhere, whether we be in Jerusalem, Samaria, or the ends of the earth. But when we have resolved to live beyond the shores of our own existence and live for others, we are missionaries wherever we wake up that morning.

Who is the "one another" we should prefer? I believe that is simply each other, our neighbor, the one we are called to love as we love ourselves. More specifically, the one Jesus wants us to give preference to is the one who does not yet know Him. That is the single parent who is now coming to the church for the first time with his or her kids; that is the elderly man or woman who deserves to be welcomed by a great hosting team. The Bible says that when this one responds to Jesus, the Head, because of how well Jesus, the Body, took care of them, there is great rejoicing in Heaven. Let's see how our God responds to the one who turns to Him.

> *I tell you that in the same way there will be more rejoicing in heaven over one sinner who repents than over ninety-nine righteous persons who do not need to repent* (Luke 15:7 NIV).

So, according to this verse, while we may get excited over what happens in the whole of our service, Heaven gets more excited in those closing moments when the one lost or backslidden person responds. How we choose to live beyond ourselves in our local church actually lays the platform for the lost ones to come and respond to Him.

Not only should each member of the church think evangelistically concerning their local community, the church as a local body should also have programs of care that demonstrate God's love in practical ways to people in need throughout the week. Social action, humanitarian help, feeding programs, and prison and hospital visiting are some of those ways, to name a few. What are the needs in your local area for which you can be the very practical hands and feet of Jesus on a regular basis?

- Who is in your Jerusalem (your local, everyday mission field)?

- How can you make Jesus known to them and bring them to Him?

- What teams in church do you need to become a part of? *(Remember good intentions produce nothing; ring your pastor or church today and get yourself on a team if you are not already.)*

- What practical projects can you be involved with to demonstrate God's love to people in your local world?

SAMARIA AND JUDEA

This area represents your national sphere. The Church has a responsibility to train and release people to be involved in God's business in their nation. For me, that is Great Britain. How can we *go* to our nation? One of the ways we can *go* is to bless and partner with other churches and ministries that are doing something for God nationally. Having a heart to be involved with things happening in your nation extends your boundaries; it is a commitment to seeing the bigger picture of what God is doing in the land in which you live. I believe this is primarily a matter of changing the way we think. Do you think that the boundaries of the church you're called to end with what your church is doing locally—or do you see that the Church is God's Body working in every nation?

As a church, we have always been committed to partnering with other churches and ministries in the UK, helping however we can to develop synergy and introduce people to Jesus. Often our support in this sphere is through praying for, and giving to, other ministries—but when the opportunity arises, we need to be ready to help in practical ways. When it comes to assisting and partnering with others in our nation, I think we should come at a run. This readiness comes from the understanding that, if we help others to score a goal, it is a common win because we are one Body. I believe we are in a crucial time—a time when we will see small independent churches, which have chosen to live isolated lives, and do their own thing, either close their doors or branch out and begin to find healthy relationships with other ministers and ministries that carry a common culture and passion for Jesus. When they do this, they will produce a synergy beyond what they have imagined. We are living in a time when there will be many networks and alliances formed between formerly independent churches, many of them crossing what were once rigid denominational barriers. God is calling His Body to come together for a common purpose; it will soon no longer matter who is in charge, only that we get the job done for God together.

THE ENDS OF THE EARTH

As a group of mission-minded go-ers for God, we need to be effective not only in our local and national spheres of influence, but also throughout the world. Once again, this can involve our praying, giving, or going—and sometimes all of the above. I think it is vital for every local church to have healthy connections to the things that God is doing in other places around the world, especially in the non-western areas where there can be so many needs. I personally believe that it is also good for every believer to go on short-term mission trips. In doing so, they expose themselves to people and needs outside of their natural "habitat." Seeing photos is not the same as being personally touched by the needs and pains of people in other places. Those experiences can define you for the rest of your life in a positive way. They also give the opportunity for the local church to be a blessing to other churches and projects that so appreciate it across the globe. It provides the local church with an awareness of the needs of their brothers and sisters in other places and then places a responsibility on them to do something about the needs they now know about. Every time I go on a mission trip, it always ends up costing the church and me, because I come back with information about a project or a person who needs our support and subsequently receives it.

> *But whoever has this world's goods, and sees his brother in need, and shuts up his heart from him, how does the love of God abide in him?* (1 John 3:17)

I have noticed that whenever I have taken people with me to the Philippines or Africa, they are a great blessing, but they also come back changed. God does something in them that they never lose. We need to rediscover the marching orders of the early Church and move from being settlers to being go-ers, responding to this common commission as they did when they first heard it. Let's face it; we should do "greater things" now because we have planes, trains, and automobiles. As we return to missional-minded thinking, I believe we actually return to that which God loves and has ordained for us to do. When we read what God says to the church in Ephesus (when He first commends them for what they have done and then rebukes them for losing their first love), we often miss the very next thing that He says:

> *Yet I hold this against you: You have forsaken the love you had at first. Consider how far you have fallen!* **Repent and do the things you did at first** (Revelation 2:4-5 NIV).

Essentially, He says, "Return to Me, your first love, and do the things you did at first." The New King James Version says, "Return and do the first works." God was speaking to the early Church. What were those first works to which they were called to return? I believe they were the things they first valued, the things that were on the blueprint that Jesus gave them. Central to that blueprint is the great commission: they were a people who loved to live beyond the shores of their own existence, who loved to carry the message that would change people's lives. As Paul so simply said, "How will they know if they do not hear?"

> *As Scripture says, "Anyone who believes in Him will never be put to shame." For there is no difference between Jew and Gentile— the same Lord is Lord of all and richly blesses all who call on Him, for, "Everyone who calls on the name of the Lord will be saved." How, then, can they call on the one they have not believed in? And how can they believe in the one of whom they have not heard? And how can they hear without someone preaching to them? And how can anyone preach unless they are sent? As it is written: "How beautiful are the feet of those who bring good news!"* (Romans 10:11-15 NIV)

These verses lay out for us a very simple equation concerning how lost people (those who have not heard and responded to the good news of Jesus) get to experience salvation:

1. All people who call on the name of the Lord will be saved.

2. How can they call on someone they have not believed in?

3. How can they believe in someone they have not heard about?

4. How can they hear about Jesus if no one tells them about Him?

5. How can people tell them about Him if they are not equipped and sent to do so?

Paul finishes by stating how beautiful the feet are of those who are mission-minded, who leave the boundaries of their own lives every day with the intention of making the good news of Jesus known to those who do not yet know. I love how this process of salvation reads in the Message translation:

> *But how can people call for help if they don't know who to trust? And how can they know who to trust if they haven't heard of the One who can be trusted? And how can they hear if nobody tells them? And how is anyone going to tell them, unless someone is sent to do it? That's why Scripture exclaims, A sight to take your breath away! Grand processions of people telling all the good things of God!* (Romans 10:14-17 TM)

I love the way that finishes: "*Grand processions of people telling all the good things of God!*" That is a great picture of God's blueprint commission being fulfilled. This is what our world needs. Whether it be local, national, or international, the world needs people carrying (like the donkey that Jesus loosed) the person and the message of Jesus, and the salvation He brings. This leaves the Church in the 21st century with a very real challenge. How much do we want people to hear about, and experience, salvation? How will they hear unless someone goes?

AND FINALLY

Let us not leave the great commission half unpacked. It commissions us to go, taking the message of Christ to every sphere of influence in our lives, but also to go in power—liberating people from what binds them.

> *And these signs will follow those who believe: In My name they will cast out demons; they will speak with new tongues; they will take up serpents; and if they drink anything deadly, it will by no means hurt them; they will lay hands on the sick, and they will recover* (Mark 16:17-18).

For far too long now, much of the modern-day Church has left this part of the great commission politely out, yet Jesus clearly said that there would be signs that follow people who believe. They would...

- Cast out demons.

- Speak with new tongues.

- Supernaturally deal with things that have the potential to kill and hurt them.

- Lay hands on the sick and see them recover.

Each of these signs would be worthy of a chapter—suffice it to say we have been sent out with more than a message. We have been given His name and authority over things that harm, restrict, and imprison people. We are to lay hands on the sick and bear witness to the One who still heals. We are to release those who are bound by the wicked plans of the devil. Jesus has placed His Spirit on us, and in us, to release people from captivity, not just to lead them to Heaven. The same Spirit that was in Jesus is now in us. It is vital to know, as we re-embrace the great commission and purpose in our hearts to go, that we are being sent, empowered by Him, to make a difference. We need to arise and unroll the scroll over our lives, as Jesus did over His own life in Luke 4, and proclaim with God-given confidence these same words:

> And He was handed the book of the prophet Isaiah. And when He had opened the book, He found the place where it was written: "The Spirit of the LORD is upon Me, because He has anointed Me to preach the gospel to the poor; He has sent Me to heal the brokenhearted, to proclaim liberty to the captives and recovery of sight to the blind, to set at liberty those who are oppressed; to proclaim the acceptable year of the LORD" (Luke 4:17-19).

Enough talking, let's get walking—*Go!*

5

DISCIPLESHIP REVISITED

And Jesus came and spoke to them, saying, "All authority has been given to Me in heaven and on earth. Go therefore and make disciples of all the nations, baptizing them in the name of the Father and of the Son and of the Holy Spirit" (Matthew 28:18-20).

W e have spoken about being equipped for the works of the ministry, as well as the need for the 21st-century Church to re-embrace the great commission and the commandment of Jesus to *go*. Let us now consider what we are to do when we go. The verses above teach us that we are to "go and make disciples of all nations," but how do we do that? What is a disciple? And what does effective discipleship actually look like in the modern Church?

DISCIPLESHIP TAKES THE NEXT STEP

Have you noticed that Jesus never actually said to His Church, "Go and get people saved," but rather, "Go and make disciples"? Being an evangelist for many years, I read "great commission" verses through the filter of my calling: "Go do meetings, preach Jesus, and get as many to respond to the good news of the Gospel as you possibly can." Now, this is not wrong, but it's not what the great commission of Jesus fully asks us to do. Of course, that first step that people take when they believe in Jesus as Lord and Savior is a vitally important one. The moment they take that initial step, powerful things occur in their lives, according to Scripture:

- All of their sins are forgiven; as far as east is from west, they are removed.

- They become friends of God because all enmity and every argument that once separated them from God are fully settled.

- They gain an inherited, unearned righteousness that leaves them holy, justified, and righteous in the sight of their God.

- They become born again, or born anew; an old creation dies and a new resurrected life in Christ begins.

- They become citizens of His commonwealth and a member of His household; they become heirs with the Father and co-heirs with the Son.

- They no longer have to fear hell, but can have a perfect assurance that when the currency of the days of this life is spent, they will be present with God in Heaven for all eternity.

All of this, and much more besides, occur in that single moment a person believes in Jesus as Lord. Maybe you are thinking, *Surely it must take a longer process to achieve all of that!* Well, think about the thief on the cross; how long did he have? Minutes...seconds?

> *One of the criminals who hung there hurled insults at Him: "Aren't You the Messiah? Save Yourself and us!" But the other criminal rebuked him. "Don't you fear God," he said, "since you are under the same sentence? We are punished justly, for we are getting what our deeds deserve. But this man has*

*done nothing wrong." Then he said, "Jesus, remember me when You come into Your kingdom. **Jesus answered him, "Truly I tell you, today you will be with Me in paradise."** It was now about noon, and darkness came over the whole land until three in the afternoon, for the sun stopped shining. And the curtain of the temple was torn in two. Jesus called out with a loud voice, "Father, into Your hands I commit My spirit." When He had said this, He breathed His last* (Luke 23:39-46 NIV).

As you can see in verse 46, this conversation took place in the closing moments of Jesus' earthly life. We do not know exactly what the man had done, but, unlike Jesus, he actually deserved to be there and is referred to as "the other criminal." Since crucifixion was the worst punishment given, we would be right to suppose this man in his life had done some pretty bad things. Notice he does not claim his innocence even once during the conversation; rather, he admits that he and the other man deserve to be there. While the other criminal pours insults upon Jesus, this man speaks up in His defense and then makes a powerful faith-based confession, asking to be remembered in paradise. Listen again to the response of Jesus: "With truth I tell you, today you will be with Me in paradise." Notice that He did not say, "Sorry, Charlie, you left it too late"; neither did He sentence him to any penance or a series of Hail Marys or any other man-made ordinance. No, He simply responded to the thief's plea for salvation by saying, "It's done; be assured, you are going to be there with Me today." What? No counselling, deliverance, or preparation courses? No. Simply faith. By faith, this man entered into the abundant grace of God and was saved, and so are we when we believe in Jesus. This is the blessed assurance that God's Word gives us regarding the salvation we have received from Him. That first step of believing in Jesus is a powerfully important one. It is a step that totally redefines who we are, with eternal ramifications for our lives.

THEY MAY BE SAVED, BUT ARE THEY CHANGED?

In that moment of salvation, we know that, by God's doing, we become spiritually alive (born anew) as the triune (three-part) creation we were originally designed by God to be: alive to God now in body, soul, and spirit. We know that, because eternity has now entered into our hearts, we will never fully die again (see Eccles. 3:11). Though the body we currently live in will one day give up and die, we will not, and we are guaranteed new glorified bodies that await us beyond the grave. So, our spirits are made alive again; we get new glorified bodies in Heaven, but what about our souls? By soul, I mean that place that we have always lived out from, the control center that stores all the information, memories, and emotions of our lives.

Is the soul or mind of a person changed in that moment of salvation? Do we suddenly not have any recollection of things that have previously happened to us? The answer, obviously, is of course not. Though our whole lives are now fully paid for and redeemed, our souls remain unchanged. That first step of salvation is indeed like a divine car wash that washes our sins totally away, but not the contents of our souls. At salvation, God does not erase all the information that has been stored on the hard disk of your life, nor does He rid you of all the memories and emotions that have accumulated in the journey of your life. Your soul and its contents are changed by something else, and that something else is an ongoing commitment to what we commonly term "discipleship." I believe that discipleship needs to be taught as the natural and progressive next step beyond salvation. It's a commitment to discipleship that enables us to be transformed and to come into all that God has destined for us to be.

I remember making a somewhat shocking statement to my church once when I was teaching on these realities. I said, "Hey, church, I don't want you to go to Heaven saved. I love you too much for that. I want to see each of you go to Heaven one day saved and changed, with lives that have been transformed by the both the power of the Spirit, and the Word of God. A transformation that came as you committed to live a life of discipleship—not just settling for being a follower of Jesus, but becoming His disciple."

GOD WANTS TO GET BENEATH THE VENEER

Think about a kitchen counter. For wealthier people, these are often made out of granite or solid oak. For the not-so-rich, counters are more often made out of what we call in the UK "chipboard," which is basically resin-compacted wood chips/flakes. This solid, dense mass is then coated in a layer of veneer that is waterproof and wipeable. These counters, like the kitchen units that are made of the same material, are a lot cheaper than granite or oak and are great until your washing machine or dishwasher leaks. Then, like blotting paper or a wheatabix cereal bar, the chipboard soaks up the warm, soapy water. Then, your kitchen swells to ten times its normal size and needs to be replaced.

Our lives are like these countertops. We all have a coating of veneer, but beneath that veneer, is the chipboard or wood grain that makes us who we really are. God does not want to spend the rest of your life just dusting your veneer, or surface; He wants to get into the woodchip or inner part of who you are because it's from that deeper part of your life that you daily determine how you will live out your life. A true commitment to discipleship is when, after making the decision to give God ownership of the worktop (salvation), new believers then dare to let God not just dust and wipe the surface of who they are, but also have open, unlimited access into their deepest parts. They allow Him to bring all the changes to their souls—including their thoughts, emotions, and memories—that He needs to.

So, if we are to "go and make disciples," we need to realize that it is actually not just about leading people in that first step (salvation), but also having a commitment to helping them to bring God's life-changing truth and wisdom into the central world (the chipboard) of their lives.

Is true discipleship simply about putting on more meetings so that we can throw more information from the Bible at people, hoping that some of it will stick? No. I think real discipleship is more about walking with people—getting into their lives in a much deeper way, finding out what makes them tick, and then helping them to apply the truths of God's Word. True discipleship changes the inner world of a person; internal transformations will always produce external changes that last a lifetime.

DISCIPLESHIP CHANGES YOUR BELIEF SYSTEM

Whether it's a person, a city, or a nation, this principle remains the same: real long-term change is brought about only when we "stay around for a bit" and dare to change the internal belief systems that produce the daily living patterns of a person or a place.

When I used to read about the travels of the early apostles, like Paul and Peter, I pictured them turning up in a place for three nights or a week and holding a crusade—leading crowds of people to Jesus and then moving on to the next city. Perhaps that happened on occasion, but I think that, for the most part, the work of the apostles looked nothing like that. We read that they stayed in a city, reasoned, and taught the people the truth of God's Word—sometimes for years at a time; we then hear about how the whole city was radically transformed. A city like Ephesus was, when the disciples first arrived, a wicked place where most people were worshipping the goddess Diana and doing the most evil things you could imagine, including child prostitution and the ritual sacrifice of infants. But, as Paul and his team stayed and daily taught about the person of Jesus, of righteousness by faith, and God's grace, the culture of the city was radically transformed. Discipleship so altered the daily life of the city that it became a God-worshipping place where false gods, like Diana, were no longer worshipped or feared!

The disciples knew that they would experience only partial or temporary change if they did not replace the wisdom that was at the very heart of the city with something greater, so they began to impart the wisdom of God. Human wisdom was replaced with divine wisdom, and the outworking of this discipleship was new belief, transformed lives, and a lasting move of God in a once-pagan city.

It is exactly the same with our lives. We may be in a hurry, but God is not. When we commit to let His Word remain and work within us, the belief systems of our lives are truly transformed, not for a moment, but forever. I am sure that, like me, you have had enough of momentary changes. People earnestly come forward in a meeting and are wonderfully saved; they are set free from addictions and habits that have defined them too long, and, for a while, they stay free. They no longer run to the bottle or drugs like they used to. All is good. Then one day, you hear the sad news they have gone back to what they once knew. They have returned to the Egypt from which they had been so wonderfully delivered. Why? I believe that most often it is because their belief systems were never changed or renewed completely by effective discipleship, so when a moment of pressure, temptation, or opportunity arose, it was too easy to revert to those old things they once knew. It was like putting on a familiar coat they had once worn, taken off, but never actually removed from the wardrobe of their lives. The information stored in the control room of their lives had never been fully renewed, replaced, or overwritten with better information. They had taken that one vitally important step of salvation, but had never taken any further steps of discipleship. They had become saved, but not transformed.

NEW COORDINATES

Another good example we commonly use for this principle is the autopilot setting in an airplane. Before flying, the pilot enters the coordinates for his destination into the autopilot system. He then sits back, and the plane flies true to those coordinates. If, during the flight, he decides he wants to change the direction or destination, he has two choices. First, he can try to override it manually. To do this, he needs to physically grab the controls of the plane and with all his energy force them in another direction. Depending on the autopilot system, he may be able to do this for a while, but not for long. As soon as his arms get tired or he needs to scratch his nose, he will let go of the controls; the plane will instantly revert to autopilot and the coordinates originally entered into its system. His might, or current persuasion, may be able to sustain directional change for a moment, but not continually.

For directional change to happen in a way that can be sustained and absolute, he would need to reenter new coordinates into the autopilot system. When the information in the autopilot is successfully changed, the plane will naturally change course according to its new route, without the expenditure of energy needed when manually trying to override the system. This is what a commitment to discipleship does. It gets God's Word into the autopilot settings of your life and causes them to be renewed, so that you can live consistently in a new direction without having to do it by your own strength alone.

CALLED TO BE TRANSFORMED!

The Bible does not say, "Get saved and remain the same"; rather, the believer is to be transformed. God's Word teaches us that we are transformed by two specific things: the working of the Spirit of God within our lives (see 2 Cor. 3:18), and the renewing of our minds.

> *Therefore, I urge you, brothers and sisters, in view of God's mercy, to offer your bodies as a living sacrifice, holy and pleasing to God— this is your true and proper worship. Do not conform to the pattern of this world, but be transformed by the renewing of your mind. Then you will be able to test and approve what God's will is—His good, pleasing and perfect will* (Romans 12:1-2 NIV).

The renewal of the mind takes place when we dare to replace some of the information that is currently stored in it. Our current thoughts and beliefs will always determine our destination. When we dare to allow the truth of God's Word to replace anything that is not God's perfect truth, our destination is re-plotted in line with His purposes.

Your mind is just like a computer hard drive; in fact, computers at their very conception were based on how the mind of a person operates with its ability to store and process information. Now think about this: if you were to buy a used computer, it would have data programmed on it by the previous owner, and the processor within it would function in accordance with the information on the hard drive. In other words, the information stored on the computer would determine its actual potential. Whatever instruction you now tapped into the computer would be answered in accordance with its current data. What if that data was corrupt, out of date, or not suitable for what you now need? What would you have to do to get the computer to function according to your requirements? Obviously, you would have to replace the old data with new data that would then enable the computer to function as you, the new owner, desire it to do.

In the same way, when God takes ownership of our lives through that first step of salvation, He takes on a computer (a life) with old information on its hard drive—some of which is fine and will continue to work well, and some of which may negatively affect the running, potential, or future direction of the computer. That information needs to be deleted and replaced with new information that will cause the computer to work as the new owner desires. Discipleship is about allowing God to change your "stored information" as He sees necessary.

Another example is a person who makes apple pies. He or she has the potential to make the same type of pie every day simply by using the same ingredients, heat, and oven. But what if a pie does not taste good? Then, he or she needs to change the ingredients, and the pie will taste different. If the ingredients are never changed, the same pie will be produced! In the same way, God gets us, by His goodness, to repent, or "change the ingredients of the pie of our lives." (In other words, the way we think.) As we replace other pre-programmed thoughts and wisdom with His thoughts and wisdom, the flavor of the pie of our lives changes, and *remains* changed. The bottom line is always this: if you truly want to change the way you live, you always have to change the way you think!

Consider also the true essence of repentance. Repentance in the New Testament is actually more a matter of changed thinking than it is of sorrowful remorse. The word for repentance most commonly used is the Greek word *metanoia*, which means "to change one's mind or thinking"![1] This is a very different meaning from the Old Testament Hebrew word most often used for repentance *nacham*, which means "to be mournfully sorrowful."[2]

When it comes to repentance, God most desires that we change our thinking. Yes, we may feel sorrowful when we have done something wrong, and that's normal, but it should never stop there. We always need to move on to do something about the potential of it happening again. How? Only by daring to change the way we think; it is not till we dare to change the way we think, that we will change the way we live permanently. If we do not change our thinking, we set ourselves up to continue the same patterns. A sorrowful response is not a bad thing, but it needs to be the doorway into something much larger—namely a change of thinking within that specific area of our lives being highlighted by God.

> *Or do you despise the riches of His goodness, forbearance, and longsuffering, not knowing that the goodness of God leads you to repentance (change your thinking)?* (Romans 2:4)

When we reach people for Christ by revealing God's goodness and love toward them and they "repent," we need to always understand that their repentance is not about just "feeling bad about the life they have lived prior to accepting Jesus." As well as acknowledging Jesus and the new life He gives them, they must now begin to change their thinking and bring their minds into alignment with His truth. When they do these things, they gain a new life and can live out that new life to the fullest.

DEVELOPING A CORRECT PHILOSOPHY

Apparently the word *Christian* is mentioned only three times in the Bible, whereas the word *disciple* is mentioned 239 times. Maybe it's primarily important that we see ourselves as His disciples, rather than as just Christians. When you are committed to being a disciple, you are hungry for God to deal with your belief system, that inner part of you that you live from daily. The reality is that everyone has a belief system formed, for the most part, by the things we have been exposed to and the experiences we have had thus far. The environment we were raised in, the authority figures who influenced us for good or for ill, the peers we have spent our time with—all these things (and more) have determined, in one way or another, what we deem to be true and right. Often, these factors even determine what we unconsciously expect.

A very sad example of this reality is a person who has been subject to abuse of one kind or another from an early age. Maybe it was all she experienced in her formative years. Sadly, after a while, it becomes what she expects—even what she thinks she deserves. I have seen this time and time again. People who have experienced abuse early in life then find themselves moving from one abusive relationship to another; and after being abused yet again, they act as if they somehow deserved it. This is very sad and breaks God's heart. What's the problem? Often it is that, over the years, their environment has conditioned their internal belief systems concerning their worth, and what they should expect or define as normal in life. If their current definition of normal is not interrupted, it will remain their default setting.

It's not until another voice or perspective convincingly invades that deception that a way out can become a reality, or even an option, to them. I believe the message of God's Kingdom is exactly that. It's like a yellow brick road that invades the incarcerating boundaries in a person's life with an offer of a better life. The message of the Kingdom offers new beginnings and better things, not just to the abused, but to everyone who hears it.

As a pastor, when I have spent time with people who have experienced abuse, I have so often heard them say that they "probably deserved it," or that "it's what they should expect." It's amazing to see the response I get when I disagree with them and present them with truth. When I gently, but firmly, say, "You know that's rubbish. You're actually believing a lie. You don't deserve to be abused. No one does," or when I tell them, "That person had no right to do what he did to you. He was wrong, not you," suddenly the posture of the person changes, and the head lifts. What's happening? Correct thinking, or wisdom, is invading the place of deception and is offering them a way out to a more fruitful life. As I continue to underline their true God-given value and their right to be loved, they begin to embrace the new wisdom they are being exposed to, and everything begins to change.

What happened to change their wrong beliefs? Simply—truth was offered. If they accept it in place of the old lies, then there is nothing stopping them from breaking free of the prison they have always known. They will see their lives and relationships change, beyond what they ever dreamed or thought they deserved.

I'm sorry if this is a sensitive issue to some of you. I want to show you how allowing God's Word to renew your mind and change your thinking can radically change and release your life, and the life of the person that you are discipling. Dusting the countertop will bring no lasting freedom, but dealing with the root of the problem by getting God's thoughts and wisdom into the belief system of the person will cause radical, lasting change.

As I have already said, the various experiences, people, and wisdom you have so far been exposed to in life are the major ingredients forming your belief and value systems. What if some, or all, of the wisdom you have been exposed to in your life has not been true? How can you know if it is true or not? The answer may seem very narrow-minded, but it will produce the God-intended freedom we all need. You have to dare to hold it against the wisdom of God's Word to see if there is a collision of wisdoms. If there is, you then must act like a disciple and have the courage to choose God's wisdom over any of the other wisdom you may have known; then you will experience the transformations that God has promised and intended for you!

The wisdom or knowledge you are exposed to in life, especially in your formative years, becomes the wisdom and knowledge that you love or deem to be true. That loved or embraced wisdom forms the personal philosophy of your life. Your philosophy then develops your belief system, and it's from that belief system that you daily, consciously and unconsciously, live your life—unless there is an interruption, and the wisdom that fuels your personal philosophy is challenged by another, or better, wisdom.

WE ARE ALL PHILOSOPHERS

The truth is, we are all philosophers. You do not go to school or college to get a philosophy—you already have one. It is simply your system of beliefs and values that are the product of the wisdom and knowledge you have chosen to embrace as true in your life. Philosophy sounds like a difficult word, but it is actually quite simple. It is one word made up of two words: *philo* and *sophia. Philo* means "loving; having an affinity for," and *sophia* means "wisdom." When you join the two words together, it forms its actual meaning. Philosophy essentially is just "the love of wisdom." The questions remain: what wisdom are you loving? And where are you sourcing it from? Being free people who live in an apparently free world, we all have a choice regarding the wisdom we embrace, and where we obtain that wisdom. We can continue to get it from the places we knew before we knew God, or we can choose to obtain it now from God Himself. Look at what Paul says about philosophy:

Beware lest anyone cheat you through philosophy and empty deceit, according to the tradition of men, according to the basic principles of the world, and not according to Christ (Colossians 2:8).

This text gives us a clear picture that there are different sources available in life offering us wisdom to form our philosophies by; the choice of where we source it from remains with us. Will we turn to *"human traditions and the basic principles of this world,"* or will we turn to Christ and the wisdom contained within God's infallible Word? Discipleship daily chooses to make God the source of the wisdom which you embrace and love in every area of your life. You are a philosopher because you have a philosophy. Again, the questions I ask you are, what wisdom are you currently loving, and where did you personally get it from?

Wisdom is the principal thing; therefore get wisdom. And in all your getting, get understanding. Exalt her, and she will promote you; she will bring you honor, when you embrace her. She will place on your head an ornament of grace; a crown of glory she will deliver to you (Proverbs 4:7-9).

This proverb encourages us to *"get wisdom"*! There is certainly no shortage of available wisdom in our twenty-first century lives. Everyone claims to have "pure truth and genuine knowledge"—everything from evolution to humanism. There is no shortage of "stores to get some wisdom" if you are in the market to get some.

The problem is that no wisdom outside of God's is truly pure. The "other wisdom" that is being made available to you may not be evil, but it simply is not as good for you as God's wisdom is—and most of it actually finds its origins in God's original truth anyway. It is the product of people who have reworded and presented principles from the Bible as though they originated them. However, Colossians 2 actually gives us a strong warning about shopping for wisdom outside of God. Listen to the opening of the verse from three different translations:

See to it that no one takes you captive through hollow and deceptive philosophy (Colossians 2:8 NIV).

Beware lest anyone cheat you through philosophy and empty deceit (Colossians 2:8 NKJV).

Beware lest any man spoil you through philosophy and vain deceit (Colossians 2:8 KJV).

Wrong philosophy has the potential to take you captive, cheat, and even spoil you! Be careful where you go shopping. Decide to keep your philosophy pure and uncontaminated. This world does not love or acknowledge our God and His truth; it is ever-wanting to make you a "wisdom cocktail"—a bit of humanism, a bit of paganism, a shot of Christianity, and a flashy name to make you want it. It may be a funky-looking concoction, but it won't taste good to your life. In fact, it's poison to your soul. Keep it pure. Why get your wisdom from somewhere inferior, when you have the opportunity to get it from the One who makes the genuine article? There is too much "wisdom-mixing" going on, even within Christianity today, and it's time for us to look again to the blueprint, the Word of God, and say, "This alone contains the wisdom I need for every situation I may face." Get wisdom. Get God's wisdom!

RETURNING TO GOD TO GET YOUR WISDOM

If any of you lacks wisdom, you should ask God, who gives generously to all without finding fault, and it will be given to you (James 1:5 NIV).

This is one of my favorite verses. I remember when I first discovered these truths, and I have since regularly applied them to my life. They have always delivered exactly what was promised; they have caused so many breakthroughs in different areas of my life. Look closely with me at what this verse teaches us. First, the verse applies to everyone: "If any one lacks wisdom." All of us lack wisdom at one time or another.

How is it that we can be so wise in one part of our life, but at the very same time be so *unwise* in another part? Our lives, like a pizza, are a whole, but a whole that is made up of different slices. Like the image below shows, our lives have different aspects, and each of them needs God's wisdom to flourish. Effective discipleship is to give God ownership over the whole of your life (the pie), and to also daily embrace His wisdom in each and every one of the individual aspects that make you (the pie) who you are.

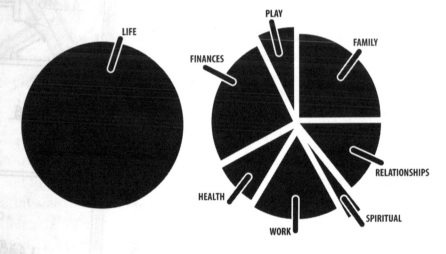

Some of the individual sections of your life needing God's wisdom include the following:

- Finances
- Health and fitness
- Work or vocation
- Spirituality
- Sexuality and morality
- Recreation and relaxation
- Relationships, with their various demands:
  - Being a parent

- Being a husband or wife

- Being a friend

Just like a pizza, these individual sections, or slices, make up the whole pie of who you actually are. I love Italian food, and when I am in an Italian restaurant, I love to sprinkle parmesan cheese on everything. Let's say that the waiter comes over and asks if I want cheese on my pizza, and I respond, "Yes, but only on specific slices. I will have it on these two slices, but not on this one or that one." The waiter would think I am crazy. But that is what we often do to God when it comes to including His wisdom in the different areas of our lives. We need to give God full access and allow His wisdom to be "sprinkled" upon every part of our lives. Then we will see transformation beyond what we believed possible in every aspect of who we are.

For those lacking wisdom, James 1:5 says, "You should ask God, who gives generously." Why do we not do this? Why do we not automatically run to God in order to get the wisdom we need? I believe we don't for a couple of reasons. First, because we know the wisdom He will give us will cause a lot of change, and maybe we don't really want the change it will cause. Second, we may think that, if we ask God for wisdom, because we have made some mistakes, He will first rebuke us, saying something like, "Before I give you wisdom, let's talk about what an idiot you have been." This is where James 1:5 is so good; God actually guarantees that He will not do this. Listen to what the verse says: "You should ask God, who gives generously to all without finding fault, and it will be given to you." Without finding fault! Listen to how other translations put these incredible truths:

> *If any of you is deficient in wisdom, let him ask of the giving God [Who gives] to everyone liberally and ungrudgingly, **without reproaching or faultfinding**, and it will be given him* (James 1:5 AMP).

If you don't know what you're doing, pray to the Father. He loves
to help. **You'll get His help, and won't be condescended to when**
you ask for it. *Ask boldly, believingly, without a second thought*
(James 1:5 TM).

What a great assurance to have! When we need His wisdom, we can approach our God, the source of true wisdom, and get an abundance of it without reproach. I believe He does not give you reproach because He knows that the wisdom you get from Him will fix what was causing the problem that made you need it. Plus, He promised to give grace to the humble (see James 4:6). To approach Him for help is to walk in the sort of humility He loves.

OTHER WISDOM WAS THE ORIGINAL PROBLEM

The offer of "another or alternative wisdom" goes right back to the Garden of Eden, and was actually what the original temptation was all about. It was not about a piece of fruit, but about an enlightenment that promised "a better wisdom than what you had." Look at the original offer that was made to Eve:

When the woman saw that the fruit of the tree was good for food
and pleasing to the eye, **and also desirable for gaining wisdom,**
she took some and ate it. She also gave some to her husband, who
was with her, and he ate it (Genesis 3:6 NIV).

Did you catch the bit in the middle? "And desirable for gaining wisdom..." Let's look at how other versions translate this section:

"A tree to be desired in order to make one wise" (AMP).

"A tree desirable to make one wise" (NKJV).

"And realized what she would get out of it—she'd know every-thing!" (TM)

The devil offered "other wisdom" to Eve because he knew that, if he could get them to take another wisdom, he could pollute or corrupt them from the inside. That new wisdom they exchanged for God's would create new philosophies that would, in time, produce alternative belief systems to continually separate them from God. Remember that the wisdom you choose to embrace will develop the philosophy that produces the belief system out of which you will end up living daily.

So we see that Adam and Eve were originally in possession of pure wisdom from God; then, they were sold another wisdom by satan. They were told that God was holding back, and that a better wisdom was available to them. They accepted his lies as truth and embraced this other wisdom. Of course, we now know that they actually gave away, on that day, the best for the least, the genuine for the counterfeit.

We need to understand that, at that moment when they turned to take the alternative wisdom from the hand of satan, they turned their back on God's pure wisdom. They could face only one person at a time. When they turned their back on God's pure wisdom, they began to receive an inferior wisdom outside of God. The good news is that we believe in a 100-percent redemption produced by Jesus; everything that was lost through Adam's foolishness was restored through Christ's obedience. That means everything! As God's children, we are now able to daily approach God for our wisdom, just as Adam and Eve originally did before they erred. When we do, He gives wisdom as promised in James 1:5—in abundance, without reproach. Just as Adam and Eve turned away from God's wisdom to receive another, now we need to daily make the decision to turn away from "another wisdom" to receive His. God's wisdom is the genuine article; it was in existence first, and, from it, all things were formed!

That's why God wants us to take the step beyond salvation and to commit to discipleship, so that He can correct our wrong beliefs and help us to move consistently in a brand-new direction. Remember, it really is wrong-believing that produces wrong-living.

God does not want you to spend your life collecting the bad fruit that your life produces; He wants to deal with the wrong root-beliefs that cause bad fruit to grow. He wants to adjust your personal philosophy by replacing some of the wisdom you have embraced that is contrary to His. The question is, will you let Him? I remember once teaching on the new creation in a drug rehabilitation center in New York. During my message, I shared on being transformed by the renewing of your mind. All of a sudden, a man who was a recovering crack addict at the facility, shouted out, "That's brain washing!" I stopped, thought about what he said, and then responded, "You're right, but let's face it: you need your mind scrubbed. Sir, you have been an addict for over 20 years, have gone through three marriages, and have a number of kids who do not want to have anything to do with you. I think you need your brain scrubbed; how about you?" Then I said, "With what I am teaching, at least you get to know Who is doing the scrubbing." He nodded in agreement, sat down, and continued to listen with a very open heart.

If we really want to change, if we really want to see all the promises of God become a reality in our lives and nations, we need to walk as disciples allowing God free access to everything we believe, always being ready to receive His wisdom and to replace other, lesser wisdom we may have formerly embraced.

So now we understand what true discipleship does. We need to have an ongoing commitment not just to lead people in an initial step of faith, but also to be ready to walk with them as they become disciples so that their lives can become transformed from the inside out, so they too can go to Heaven one day not just saved but transformed.

As we purpose to return to the blueprint and to build according to the pattern, we need to ask ourselves some honest questions. Are we going into the world "making disciples of people," or are we just "crop-dusting the crowd" with the Gospel, hoping that some of them may catch it and do something with it? I don't believe people should ever be used just to make crusade responses look good or to give evangelists something to post in their newsletters: "We had a thousand responses in our meetings!" Great. Please don't hear what I am not saying. I am so happy for each life given to God, but I also would respectfully like to know how many were positioned so they could take the next step as a disciple.

I know many fine evangelists who do exactly this. When they go to an area with the Gospel, they take the needed time to prepare local churches to be ready to care for those who take that first step of salvation in their crusades. But there are many others who seem to treat getting someone to pray the initial prayer like a numbers game. They meet, tell them about Jesus, get them to pray, and then quickly move on to another. Is a "hit and run" method the most successful way we should do evangelism? I know that sometimes we don't have a choice. We meet someone, and time is limited; we lead them to Christ and must leave before we can get them positioned in a local church. Obviously, it is better to lead them to Jesus than not to. You then trust God to position them where they need to be.

More specifically, I am talking about the mission of the local church. Do we put any emphasis on what happens after that initial prayer? Will we commit our lives to stay around a bit longer to disciple people after they have taken that first step? How about you personally? Who are you currently, personally, discipling? Is there anyone you are mentoring today, teaching them what you have learned so far from your journey with God? Or maybe the question should be, who is discipling *you?* Are you positioned in a healthy church or ministry where you can be challenged and transformed? These questions need to be answered if we are going to be people who are not only being discipled, but are also discipling others.

As we dare to return to God's blueprint for His Church, we cannot ignore this important "line" that is also drawn on it. We know how important other lines are to God—including the great commission and the power of God; having fellowship and living by faith—but what about this line? This line is also very important to God and needs to be so to His Church again. Remember what Jesus, the Designer of the blueprint for the Church, said, "Go into all the world and make disciples." Let me ask again, *are we?*

ENDNOTES

1. "Metanoia"; see http://concordances.org/greek/3340.htm.

2. "Nacham"; see http://concordances.org/hebrew/5162.htm.

6

RELEVANCE–AN ISSUE
OF FORM AND CONTENT

But mark this: There will be terrible times in the last days. People will be lovers of themselves, lovers of money, boastful, proud, abusive, disobedient to their parents, ungrateful, unholy, without love, unforgiving, slanderous, without self-control, brutal, not lovers of the good, treacherous, rash, conceited, lovers of pleasure rather than lovers of God—having a form of godliness but denying its power. Have nothing to do with such people (2 Timothy 3:1-5 NIV).

Over the last few years, much discussion has taken place concerning the subject of relevance and the modern church; indeed, the Church needs to be relevant to society without compromising itself. To me, when it comes to the subject of building churches that are both relevant and effective, it comes down simply to a matter of *form* and *content*. In this chapter, we will look at the fact that you actually need both; the Church needs to be relevant to people just as Jesus was so that they are drawn to the Church and not repelled. Furthermore, when they are drawn to your church, there needs to be content, something supernatural within our packaging that impacts and transforms them into all that God designed them to be.

IS THE BOOK THE SAME AS THE COVER?

As we journey through life, we often go by outward appearances, especially when it comes to people. But I am sure you have discovered, as I have, that sometimes, when it comes to both people and things, what you first see can be very different to what something actually is. Think about it, anyone can go into a fancy dress shop and hire a police or priest costume, but will that actually make them a policeperson or a priest? No, it merely means that the form is there, but the content is not.

It's the content of something that determines its purpose and potential. Some restaurants look great on the outside with all their signage and advertising, but when you get inside and experience the content, quality, or service, it can be a very different story. Sometimes it's like the classic saying, "You can't judge a book by its cover." We've all done this with books, haven't we? You pull a book off the shelf; it has an intriguing cover with endless endorsements by famous people, but when you read it, there is not much content at all. In fact, a couple of chapters through the book, and you discover you are done; you put it on the bookshelf with the other "one-day-I-will-finish-it" books.

Hopefully this is not your experience with this book, but this principle carries through to other things as well. People too can give out a projection of who they are, but after spending time with them, you can discover a completely different tale. A few times, I have watched a talk show when someone I liked or wanted to know a bit more about was being interviewed, often an actor or singer. I have often been disappointed at the actual pages that lay behind the public cover because it was a totally different story from what I thought it would be. Then, at other times, I have ended up admiring them more. It can cut both ways.

People are often judged by their covers because we live in a world where expectations of what strong or beautiful looks like are fed into us from a young age. I am so glad that, when God looks at us, He always looks beyond the cover we may be presenting to our true content.

In Scripture we see this happen both positively and negatively. In First Samuel 16 we read that the prophet Samuel is sent to the house of Jesse. God sends him there to select one of Jesse's sons to be anointed as the new king in place of Saul. So Samuel asks Jesse if he can meet his sons so he can determine which son God is going to select. Jesse does what is asked and lines up all of his sons before the prophet, but, for some reason, leaves David, his youngest son, in the field with the sheep.

Samuel goes down the line of sons, waiting for God to say, "It's him." The prophet knew He would, because He had sent him there for that purpose. He walks slowly past each of these young, strong men, all apparently filled with potential, but God says, "Not him" to each candidate. Samuel gets to the end of the line; there are no more sons, and Samuel has not heard God say, "Yes" yet.

So Samuel asks Jesse if he has any more sons. Jesse then reveals that his youngest boy, David, is out in the fields, and he sends for him to come. The moment Samuel sees the young shepherd boy he hears God say, "Yes." When others saw a shepherd boy, God saw a king. Why? Because God always looks at the content, not just at the outward appearance. Listen to how God puts it:

> But the LORD said to Samuel, "Do not consider [Eliab's] appearance or his height, for I have rejected him. The LORD does not look at the things people look at. **People look at the**

outward appearance, but the LORD looks at the heart" (1 Samuel 16:7 NIV).

This moment of appointment and anointing worked out very positively for David because God was looking beyond the outward appearance. Now let's look at this principle again worked out in a more negative way with a situation involving the Pharisees.

At the same time that Jesus was walking around Israel, the Sadducees and Pharisees were also. They were religious leaders who were meant to represent God on the earth and be His spokesmen to Israel. Amazingly, they did not recognize their "employer," God, when He came to the earth to save it. Their love of the law and the traditions of their fathers blinded so many of them that they could not see or perceive the promised Savior even when He was in the same room with them.

This blindness was in itself an issue of form and content because they were trying to know Jesus by His cover and not by His content. They saw the son of a carpenter, a boy who had grown up near them, an apparently spiritually uneducated, everyday person. How could He possibly be God's Son? Yet when God the Father looked at Him, He saw exactly that: His own begotten Son and Heaven's redemptive master plan for saving humanity. Covers can be strange things.

For many of the Pharisees of that day, the issue of cover and content was a massively personal one. They daily paraded around, dressed up in religious uniforms, performing religiously on the streets for all to see. Many of the people were totally taken in by the outward covers and performances of these people, but Jesus was not because He could see who they really were, just as God had seen who David the shepherd boy really was. Listen to Jesus' verdict concerning the scribes and Pharisees' conduct:

Woe to you, scribes and Pharisees, hypocrites! For you cleanse the outside of the cup and dish, but inside they are full of extortion and self-indulgence. Blind Pharisee, first cleanse the inside

of the cup and dish, that the outside of them may be clean also.
Woe to you, scribes and Pharisees, hypocrites! For you are like
whitewashed tombs which indeed appear beautiful outwardly,
but inside are full of dead men's bones and all uncleanness.
Even so you also outwardly appear righteous to men, but inside
you are full of hypocrisy and lawlessness (Matthew 23:25-27).

If you think I am being harsh on them or taking what He said to them out of context, go and read the rest of this chapter, and you will see that this was only the tip of the iceberg concerning His rebuke toward them. He goes on to reprimand them regarding their behavior as church leaders. He is addressing this principle of form and content. How they appeared was not actually what they were and certainly not what they were meant to be!

How refreshing it is when the form and the content of something or someone are the same! When you buy a pie, it is lovely to find that the pie looks and tastes as good as the picture on the packaging suggested it would. Likewise, when you buy a burger, it is a happy surprise to be given a burger that actually looks like the one on the advert board above your head. Or perhaps you meet someone and after spending time with him, you come to the conclusion that he is the same person inside and out; there is a wonderful absence of hypocrisy to his life.

One thing I love about Paul is that when it came to his evangelism he knew how to be a "chameleon missionary." By that, I mean he was never scared to change his form in a positive sense to enable him to reach another sub-culture of people. He never changed his content, but he would change his form to win whoever he could. In doing so, he was never guilty of compromise but simply knew how to reach people. Listen to how he explains his ability to change his form for the purpose of leading people to Christ:

Though I am free and belong to no man, I have made myself a
slave to everyone, to win as many as possible. To the Jews I be-
came like a Jew, to win the Jews. To those under the law I became

like one under the law (though I myself am not under the law), so as to win those under the law. To those not having the law I became like one not having the law (though I am not free from God's law but am under Christ's law), so as to win those not having the law. To the weak I became weak, to win the weak. I have become all things to all people so that by all possible means I might save some (1 Corinthians 9:19-22 NIV).

SHOULD CHURCH BE RELEVANT, SUPERNATURAL, OR BOTH?

*But mark this: There will be terrible times in the last days. People will be lovers of themselves, lovers of money, boastful, proud, abusive, disobedient to their parents, ungrateful, unholy, without love, unforgiving, slanderous, without self-control, brutal, not lovers of the good, treacherous, rash, conceited, lovers of pleasure rather than lovers of God—**having a form of godliness but denying its power. Have nothing to do with such people** (2 Timothy 3:1-5 NIV).*

Here Paul gives an incredibly accurate list of prophetic signposts that reveal to us that we are living in what is termed "the last days." When we read through this list, it is quite scary to see each of the signs evident daily in our society, revealing to us that this is indeed our time to shine. But what I want to specifically draw your attention to is the final sign of the times mentioned in verse 5: "having a form of godliness but denying its power. Have nothing to do with such people."

I believe Paul prophetically foretold that in the endtimes there will be a people, or rather a Church, in existence that has "the form" of godliness, just as the Pharisees had the form of what a religious leader should look like in their day. This church Paul spoke of will have the form, but it will have no content! Let me say that again, there will be a church that has good form, even fashionable, relevant form, but it will be without true godliness and it will deny its power.

So, this church will look the part but not act the part; there will be no dimension of the Spirit or experience of the supernatural power of God in it. That is not the church I want to build or be associated with—how about you? You may be saying to yourself, "That is a hard response"; then read on to find out how Paul says we are to respond to such a people. Paul advises us to "have nothing to do" with those who deny His power.

WHY NOT HAVE BOTH?

I believe that this is an issue of God's people not settling for "either/or," but daring to have both! (I will speak more about this principle in the next chapter, "The Spiritual Leader.") The way we package church is very important. Yes, it may appeal to the soulish realm of people's lives, but it is also that which normally brings them through the doors so God can impact the spiritual realm of who they are.

We should all believe to the very center of who we are that the Church is still God's master plan and the best thing in the city; we should promote and advertise her with both excellence and taste, strategically presenting the "form" of the Church to reach the communities in which we are planted. We need, with a passion, to remove the cold, dusty, unapproachable image that much of the Church has had for far too long, which actually is more based upon victorian and medieval culture and style than that of the first Church that Jesus opened.

Take a fresh look at what your church sign says. Is it inclusive? Does it welcome and entice people to cross the threshold and check you and God out? There is a church near me that always makes me smile when I drive past. They are probably great people who are praying for the lost to come, but they have not looked at their sign recently. Underneath the church name, they have this tag line: "strict and particular." If you have never been to church, would that make you want to go in? What pictures would your mind come up with concerning what was going on behind the doors? I said to my leaders, "I want our tag line to be, 'We welcome absolutely anyone.'" We have to dare to think about how we look and sound to a generation unacquainted with either God or church. Get the paint out, and take another look at how you and your facilities appear to the people who live around you. If it fits what you're doing, get some new lights and a smoke machine and make your form the best and most authentic it can be. But also make sure that there is something powerful and supernatural underneath all that packaging, paint, and lighting effects!

When the lights and special effects are turned off and the smoke no longer lingers in the air; when the fresh, ground coffee has been served and the muffins are no longer on their highly polished trays; when the catchy media stops working or the stylish illuminated signs out front are no longer shining, is there anything left in your church that can actually impact and change a life or a city? Or have you become like the emperor in that classic children's tale who is parading through the community thinking he's dressed richly only to be exposed by the innocent voice of a child? Are you, like that emperor, naked and unaware?

Make certain that when people are drawn by the form of your church, how you look and sound and by the culture you spent so much time and energy creating, they then come into a place where God's power is evident to change lives. Be a church that releases the power of God through praise and worship and preaches the Word in power so that lives are transformed. Be a church that is not scared or too polite to pray for the sick, cast out devils, and mend broken people. Be a church that has not thrown away all things spiritual but creates a hunger and desire in its people for spiritual things— for the gifts of the Spirit, the power of God, and His presence. Be a church that has spiritual content, not just a fashionable form, lest when people unwrap your packaging, they find nothing that can actually help them.

WHERE IS YOUR CONFIDENCE FOUND?

Another thing that amazes me concerning Paul and his ministry is that, when certain people met him personally, they were actually disappointed. Take a look for yourself:

> *Do you look at things according to the outward appearance? If anyone is convinced in himself that he is Christ's, let him again consider this in himself, that just as he is Christ's, even so we are Christ's. For even if I should boast somewhat more about our authority, which the Lord gave us for edification and not for your destruction, I shall not be ashamed—lest I seem to terrify you by letters. "**For his letters**," they say, "**are weighty and powerful, but his bodily presence is weak, and his speech contemptible.**" Let such a person consider this, that what we are in word by letters when we are absent, such we will also be in deed when we are present* (2 Corinthians 10:7-11).

Paul says a number of powerful things in this passage. He opens with a great statement of wisdom that speaks to us again of form. He asks the same question we have asked ourselves in this chapter, "Do we know things by outward appearance alone?" Then he reveals that there were some people who were saying that his words and the letters he wrote were so powerful, yet, in person, he was weak and could not even speak properly. They were basically saying, "He writes well, but when you meet him, it's a massive letdown."

What was their confusion? Once again, it was one of form and content. They were judging him by his outer man, his earthen vessel, and not by his inner man, the person he really was. They determined to know him by his outer form instead of his inner content. When people meet us, are they more impressed with what we look like than by what we have to say? If so, it is the wrong way around.

In insulting Paul, they actually paid him a great compliment because his confidence was never in the potential of his earthen vessel; rather, it was in that which the vessel contained! He finally responds by saying, "If they could look beyond the outer form for a moment, they would know that I am the same when away from them as I am when I am with them, because my content never changes."

Smith Wigglesworth, the radically saved English plumber and preacher, would often say of himself that the man on the inside was a thousand times bigger than the one you could see. How about you? What are you developing, taking care of, and placing your confidence in—the form that is temporal or the content which is eternal?

So when it comes to building the Church, let us not be committed to "either/or," but rather to both; let us certainly consider our packaging and have frank conversations about how we can make our outer form more relevant—but let us not for one moment lose our content in this pursuit. Let us not draw back from being people who represent and contain God's Spirit. Let us not stop being spiritual because we fear how people may react, but let us also ask the honest question, "Are we being spiritual or just weird?"

In my experience, when there is something spiritual truly happening in the church, it does not drive people away but intrigues them; it causes them to stop and think about how powerful this God we worship really is, and to ask questions that we need to be ready to answer. I agree that we need to make the church a safe place, protecting people from the spooky and the weird, but not from the dimension of the Spirit or the power of His presence.

In protecting or playing down these things, we actually compromise ourselves in a way that God disapproves of, not man. Again, think about Jesus. Was He spiritual? Did He cause supernatural things to happen as He walked among everyday people? Did they run from Him or to Him? As He was, so are we to be on the earth today. He had wonderful balance and authenticity concerning His form and content, and so must we because we are His Body on the earth. In the next chapter, we will talk in more depth about the spiritual content that these earthen vessels should contain.

7

THE SPIRITUAL LEADER

When the day of Pentecost came, they were all together in one place. Suddenly a sound like the blowing of a violent wind came from heaven and filled the whole house where they were sitting. They saw what seemed to be tongues of fire that separated and came to rest on each of them. All of them were filled with the Holy Spirit and began to speak in other tongues as the Spirit enabled them (Acts 2:1-4 NIV).

In my final chapter, I want to speak about the Church and God's people being *spiritual*. Let us never forget that the Church is not just another organization on the earth. Rather it is a spiritual organism, a living thing. Yes, we must function with the proficiency and excellence of a well-run organization, but we must always remember we are much, much more than that. The Church is the living Body of Christ on the earth, and God lives in us and works through us. We are all individually living stones, alive because of His Spirit now resident in us; built together, we make the Church that God loves and believes in (see 1 Pet. 2:5). In this chapter, let us think again about that first Church that Jesus opened; let us remind ourselves that it was born in fire, baptized in the Spirit. Each and every living stone of it on that first day was infused with power from on high, equipped and empowered to be a world changer.

When we consider the blueprint of Jesus for His Church, let us not dare to leave out the fact that we are spiritual people. The Church is not just an organization, but a *spiritual* organization, and through us, the Church, God's Spirit still moves and speaks. Our communities, now more than ever, need us to be the spiritual people, the leaders that God has always purposed for us to be. As you read this final chapter, I pray that you would be stirred and encouraged again to remember that you and your church are spiritual. Why? Because God lives in you.

> At **the** *center of all this, Christ rules* **the church. The church, you see,** *is not peripheral to* **the** *world;* **the** *world is peripheral to* **the church.** *The* **church** *is Christ's body, in which He speaks and acts, by which He fills everything with His presence* (Ephesians 1:22-23 TM).

I don't know about you, but I remain ever conscious that God has placed me on the earth for a purpose and that He made no mistakes concerning where He has placed me or when He chose to do it. Why are we here? What is it that God wants us to be to this generation that has lost its direction? The answer is a leader but, more than that, I believe we are called and positioned to be not just leaders, but spiritual leaders: to serve the purposes of God in our generation, and to realize, like Esther in her generation, that we have been born and positioned for such a time as this. In this chapter, I want to challenge all believers to see themselves and their call to spiritual leadership from God's viewpoint.

Let me say this again, He has not called you to be a leader; leadership in itself is a great call, but it's far less than God's plans for you. He has called you, destined you, to be a spiritual leader. My attention was drawn to this thought a while ago when I was reading a paper on a Saturday morning. As I skimmed over the different stories, my eyes were drawn to a quotation from a local vicar concerning an incident that had recently happened in his community. The paper introduced him this way, "… and their spiritual leader had this to say on the matter…"

My attention was caught by that statement, and I began to ponder the title that the paper had given this local vicar. They did not call him a leader, not even a community leader; they had chosen the superior title, "spiritual leader." At that moment, I saw something afresh: "Wow, imagine that! I am a spiritual leader on this earth and to my community."

Since then, I have given much thought to this term and have come up with some challenging, provoking, and, hopefully, inspiring thoughts concerning this reality. I want to challenge you to understand your call to be a spiritual leader in your world, to accept your title, to arise and be exactly that. Also, I want to explain and underline why your family, community, city, and indeed, world need you to be the spiritual leader that God is calling you to be.

NOT EITHER/OR, BUT BOTH/AND

One of the things I really don't like in life is what I call "either/or" thinking where people continually say to themselves, "Shall I have this, or shall I have that?"; "Shall I do this, or shall I do that?" There are certainly times when we have to be absolute and choose one or the other, but many times we can opt for a better solution. That solution very simply is this: you don't always have to settle for either/or; sometimes you can actually have both/and!

Sadly, this "either/or" thinking seems to be so at home within the rationale of modern-day churches; we actually need to begin to throw it out. How many times are questions like, "Shall we do this, or shall we do that?" asked? Here's a fresh question for our leadership meetings: "Can we not do both?" I am not talking about compromise; I am talking about balance. We need to be people who understand the power of synergy; sometimes things working together rather than independently can produce far better and bigger results. In everyday life, we see the power of things working together and what their synergy produces. Think of Laurel and Hardy: both were needed to make the impact they did in comedy. Consider the great culinary delight of British fish and chips: individually, they are great, but together they are an incredible delight to the taste buds. With Laurel and Hardy, fish and chips, and countless other examples, we see the power of synergy at work: things that work better together, producing more than they could if they were on their own.

The word *synergy* comes from the Greek word *synergia,* meaning joint work and cooperative action. There are many modern definitions for synergy, such as this one: "The interaction of two or more agents or forces so that their combined effect is greater than the sum of their individual effects."[1] To put it another way, synergy happens when "the whole (that which is produced) is greater than the sum of its parts (the things that are involved)."

The Bible teaches the principle of synergy in this way: one can put a thousand to flight, but two can put ten thousand to flight (see Deut. 32:30). So...when two individual people or things work together for a common purpose, they increase their potential from 1,000 to 10,000.

Now, when I went to school, they clearly taught me in math class that one plus one equals two. Yet synergy (things working together for common good) actually defies this equation and offers a far better result. Think about the fact that one can put a thousand to flight but two can put ten thousand to flight. Where did the other eight thousand come from? That's the power of synergistic relationships! They multiply our effect almost magically. Together, we leave the realms of addition for the realms of multiplication. That is why I chose the name Synergy for our network and movement of churches; it is the concept of synergy that I want the churches that partner with us to experience. As individual churches make the choice to work together for the common purpose of establishing the Kingdom of God on the earth, our effect will be multiplied far beyond what we might have achieved on our own.

In life, sometimes "either/or" thinking is actually your enemy, not your friend, as it can cause you to separate elements that work so much more effectively when they are left together. It's like walking into an office and separating two people who have great teamwork and synergy; you will still have an individual effect from them both, but nothing like you would have had if you had kept them together.

SOMETIMES YOU CAN HAVE BOTH

One of the greatest revolutions that ever came to Great Britain was the "all-you-can-eat buffet." That's right, that good, old "American way of eating." Prior to this in England, all we had was "either/or" thinking when it came to eating out. All we had was the village pub or café where the waitress would come and ask you, "What would you like? The pork, chicken, or beef?" I don't know about you, but sometimes I didn't want one or the other; I wanted some of each. At that time, however, restaurant culture would not accommodate such a revolutionary thought. So I would make my choice and then have to live with it. And so often, when everyone's food arrived, I found myself wanting what someone else had chosen! Then, all of a sudden, it arrived: the "all-you-can-eat buffet." This revolution of culinary delight defied the traditional rules of village pub mentality; it said, "You don't have to have either/or; you can have both/and." It even dared to say, "Come on, try it. Both can work together very well."

I can remember first encountering this when I lived in New York. I was driving down the road and saw the sign, "All you can eat for five bucks." Yep, you are right; I stopped and became a supporter from that day on, putting on a lot of weight very quickly. In hindsight, I now understand that my main problem was that it took me too long to work out that the sign, "All you can eat," was an invitation, not a personal challenge. Coming from the land of small portions, I thought they were throwing down the gauntlet when, in fact, they were just being nice. I have worked that out now—though I'm still a few pounds heavier.

At the risk of making you even hungrier, consider the carvery revolution. Years ago, you selected your choice from the menu and then ate it. Then came the carvery experience where you got to queue up, holding a very hot plate, to get exactly what you wanted to eat from a man wearing a white hat, holding a carving knife, and standing behind a mobile, stainless-steel unit. Still, when standing in this queue, you would encounter conditioned people who had never left the mind-set of "either/or" behind. When asked what they wanted, they would choose just one option: beef, pork, or ham. Then my turn arrived, and, with a childish grin, I would respond to the chef who was ready to carve with, "I'll have some of everything, please."

A wave of shock, even anger, would suddenly sweep from those who stood in front of me, those who had gone before. You could hear them thinking, *Who is this Oliver Twist who dares to ask for more?* As the chef calmly nodded and carried out my wishes, anger brewed in the hearts of those who had gone before. But you see, they had had their turn; they blew it, and there was no rewind. Their "either/or" thinking had left them with a lesser experience upon their plates. And behind me, a revolution started to take place as one after another, people began to shake off their pre-conditioning and recite my words, "Yep, me too. I'll have both; I'll have a piece of each." I left the carvery a rebel to those who were in front of me, yet a culinary hero to those who followed my lead: a carvery revolutionary!

I have painted that picture for you to make a point: when it comes to God, we should not live continually in an "either/or" mode of thinking; rather, we should develop a taste for synergy, a mode of thinking that says, "Sometimes I can have both; sometimes both works better and produces so much more."

Many of the things we are trying to choose from actually work very well together, and sometimes, when left together, they produce the reaction we really needed or truly desired. Remember the science lab at school and the experiments we were taught? Often they would take two different chemicals that did not do that much on their own and put them together. During their fusion, the desired reaction would occur—to the total amazement of the closely watching class. Sometimes it is when we allow things to work together that we actually get the results we have longed for. I am not talking about compromise, but synergy.

EMBRACING YOUR IDEALS AND REALITIES

Another great example involves embracing both your ideals and realities in life and ministry. Time and time again, I have seen ministers who seem resigned to accept either one or the other. I have met some who only have time for their ideals: everything has to be perfect; everything has to be on time and exactly as it "should" be. Then I have met others who can only embrace the realities of their present moment. These people can't, or won't, dare to imagine anything better, anything changed, improved, or more ideal.

Living in either of these limited viewpoints will cause you to live and lead from an unbalanced perspective. In my experience, successful leaders, whether church or corporate, need to be able to touch base with both. They need to be able to embrace their present realities in any given situation while, at the very same moment, embrace their ideals for that same situation. Their ideals help to drive them forward, to possess what they really desire, while their ability to embrace their realities will keep them from discouragement, disappointment, and disillusionment.

I heard someone say once that it is only when a person can embrace both his present realities and his future ideals that a healthy tension of effectiveness in his life or ministry is created. I like that: being able to live in the middle of what you are presently experiencing and what you really want; that tension of present reality keeps you moving to a greater and higher place.

If you understand how to balance things correctly, you can move on from "either/or" thinking to "both/and" thinking. I remember early on in the ministry, I wanted, as most ministers did, the classic Pentecostal statue of the eagle to take center place on my desk to inspire me daily (and because everyone else I knew had one!). Things have changed these days. Now, if you were going to buy me a gift for my desk, I would say, "Don't buy me an eagle. I don't have a problem motivating myself to soar; rather, buy me a set of scales to remind me to always hold all things in correct balance without compromise."

When I consider the universe and creation itself, I see all things held together with incredible balance. The air we breathe is not one single component but a perfect mixture of oxygen and nitrogen; together, they cause us to have the stuff we need to breathe. The sun, moon, stars, gravity—we are surrounded by such a well-designed, synergistic balance. In fact, sometimes the most unbalanced things on the planet seem to be some Christians with their strange, out-of-balance teachings, beliefs, and doctrines, men and women who choose to live in the ditches of "either/or" extremes rather than travel with consistency upon the central highway of truth.

I have laid this platform concerning "either/or" versus "both/and" to enable us to go a little deeper as we think about spiritual leadership. I want to challenge you to a new place of balance—to be "both/and" rather than "either/or." Being a spiritual leader is made up of these two great components, each equally important to your overall effect; one element is spirituality, and the second element is leadership.

WHEN BEING A LEADER IS NOT ENOUGH!

There are many great leaders on the earth today. Some of them know God; some don't. What I want to underline again is this simple thought: being a great leader is not enough!

Over the last few years, I have personally pursued leadership from a desire to be the best leader that I can be for God. I have read many books, listened to many tape sets, and attended, like you, many conferences that focused on the subject of leadership. None of this was wrong as my leadership potential had to increase to new levels so that I could lead and manage effectively what God has entrusted to me. But one of my own conclusions, or resolutions, that came from this "leadership" pilgrimage was this: after discovering what leadership is and what it could produce, I found that it was actually not enough for me. It did not give me what I needed to live the life I have been called by God to live. My conclusion? I don't want to be a *good* leader; that is not enough. I want to be a *spiritual leader*.

Dear friend, God has not called you to be just a leader either; He has called you to something much greater, something that is so much more effective to a dying world. He has called you to be a spiritual leader, a person who excels in natural leadership skills and abilities and who also is spiritual to the central core of who he or she is. He has called you not just to be a person who can share the wisdom, principles, and concepts that cause people to be inspired, encouraged, and motivated to great effect, but also someone who can hear God and release the power of God into a situation when principles and concepts are simply not enough. He has called you to be someone who can dispense the power and potential of God into a person's life and varied situations in times of need.

The key for effective Christian leadership is to find the right balance concerning good management and spirituality.

There really is room for both in the life of a leader and in a healthy church. In my opinion, it is the presence of both that actually makes a church healthy and effective. You need to realize in your heart that being a good leader, even if you understand every leadership principle that was ever invented, is not enough! It's good, but it's not enough. God wants you to excel in the spiritual part of the God-given title too.

As with the science lab examples we used earlier, spirituality and leadership don't contend with one another; they are not opposing magnetic forces. In fact, they were made for each other—a match made in Heaven. One actually serves and empowers the other. These individual components, each with their own unique effectiveness, work perfectly together in the life of a person or a church that loves God.

REDISCOVERING OUR SPIRITUALITY

Like many of you, I have observed with interest over the last few years the pendulum swing between leadership and the power of God within modern-day Christianity. In studying church history, I have seen that, time and time again, church people have always been so resolute on embracing one or the other—"either/or"—but fewer people have had the courage or wisdom to try and embrace both when it is possible. This is the very essence of what I am challenging you with in this chapter.

We cannot afford to have an "either/or" mentality when it comes to this issue; it is vital that we have a heart that embraces the ongoing development and health of both. This generation needs us to be people who lead and manage well, but they also need us to be people who know how to flow in the power of God. Let's face some truth here; the bottom line is that the pendulum within the Christian leader's life must actually be able to touch both parts if he or she wants to be consistently effective in leading and doing God's business on the earth!

It was not so long ago that the Church was entirely driven by "being good at being spiritual." The problem was that, although it was certainly good at that, when it came to leadership and good management, the Church was terrible at it, almost embarrassingly so. The leaders of those days did not understand much at all about good management and effective leadership; consequently, what they gained through being spiritual, they would quickly lose through mismanagement, not understanding how to lead or maintain things correctly. The Church then was indeed great at being "spiritual" with their long prayer meetings and such but, when it came to being the leaders God called them to be, they were not so clever. The pendulum was most certainly stuck on spiritual!

Then, thanks to God's goodness, a new wind began to blow, and over the last few years, a fresh emphasis was placed upon the importance of good leadership within the church. It was truly needed. Suddenly, many of us swung like the pendulum in a grandfather clock with great hunger and zeal to learn everything we could about being the leaders God had called us to be. Again, I underline: *this was so needed* and all good. Every book seemed to be about leadership; every seminar and conference was now about becoming a better leader and raising good leaders. I believe that the Lord was bringing us into a place of better balance, but it was never meant to be the final destination. It was meant to help us develop in the area of leadership so that our spirituality could be even more effective.

The worst thing we can do, however, is to embrace good leadership alone; that was never God's long-term intention in bringing us a "revival" in leadership thinking. His intention was for us to rediscover something that was needed (leadership) to empower what we already had (spirituality) so that they would work together in a synergistic unity, producing the results that His Kingdom needs.

I honestly believe that the leaders who will lead with the greatest success and impact in this next generation will be the ones who are committed to great leadership but also committed to being the spiritual people God has called them to be. Let me define that more clearly: the people who will lead with most impact are those who know how to live in, stir up, and release the power of God in their everyday lives and situations—not just lead well. I am not knocking great leadership training; I still love it myself—but there is a fresh call going throughout the earth for us to arise not just as good leaders, but as great spiritual leaders.

WHAT DO I MEAN BY SPIRITUAL?

OK, we have now established the idea that our gift to this earth is for us to arise as the spiritual leaders God has called us to be—we should not settle for being just a great leader or being just spiritual; we should be able to touch both parts of the title at any given time. Let me now better describe what I mean by *spiritual* when I speak about being spiritual leaders. The best way for me to describe what I mean by being a spiritual leader is probably to let you know first what I don't mean. By spiritual, I *don't* mean being weird and wacky, scaring others away with stupid or freaky behavior. We need to be people who are able to recognize that there is more to us—who we really are—than mere flesh and blood or natural ability. There is so much more to us and our potential than meets the natural eye.

How we choose to perceive ourselves will always determine how we live out our lives. What we think of ourselves determines many things: how we act, what we will attempt. Our behavior is always fundamentally rooted in what we believe to be true. If we consider ourselves just to be natural people or natural leaders, then the outworking of our lives and leadership will be in accordance with that belief. That is, simply put, wrong thinking. Look at Paul's message, or wake-up call, to the Corinthian church concerning their perceptions:

> *And I, brethren, could not speak to you as to spiritual people but as to carnal, as to babes in Christ. I fed you with milk and not with solid food; for until now you were not able to receive it, and even now you are still not able; for you are still carnal. For where there are envy, strife, and divisions*

among you, ***are you not carnal and behaving like mere
men?*** (1 Corinthians 3:1-3)

The apostle Paul visits this relatively newborn church in Corinth and
finds a bunch of believers acting as if nothing spiritual had happened.
They were still tangled up in the webs of envy, jealousy, and strife. He
does a couple of very profound things. First, he brings to their attention
their spiritual dietary problems. At this point, they should have been eating a juicy sirloin or T-bone steak; instead, they had settled for chocolate
milkshake. He then tells them that he can't speak to them as spiritual yet,
only as carnal. He basically calls them a bunch of nursing babies that are
too old to still be on the breast. But then we see the wisdom of Paul; he
does not focus on the symptoms but goes to the very root of the problem (the wrong belief). He asks them this very important and profound
question: "Why are you behaving like mere men?"

Look at how a couple of other translations put that question:

*Are you not unspiritual and of the flesh, behaving yourselves after
a human standard and like mere (unchanged) men?* (AMP)

Aren't you living like people of the world? (NLT)

Or, for you more traditional readers, let's look at Young's literal
translation:

Are ye not fleshly, and in the manner of men do walk?

So Paul accuses them of acting like mere men; worldly, fleshly, unchanged people. For Paul to accuse them of that, it meant that there
had to be an alternative; otherwise, it would have been unfair, even
unjust. There was an alternative, and he next leads them by the hand
into it because he understands that their behavior is the result of a fundamental misunderstanding of who they really were.

Let's look further in that same chapter as Paul reveals their true,
God-given identity to them next. Remember, this is the same chapter, same conversation; no one has taken a coffee break—same people,

same meeting, same topic. He reveals to them that they are actually temples: "Do you not know that you are the temple of God and that the Spirit of God dwells in you?" (1 Cor. 3:16)

What Paul revealed to them was that they were not actually mere men, as they had perceived themselves to be, but God-filled temples; they were actually walking, talking temples of God on the face of the earth. Look at how the Amplified Bible puts it:

> Do you not discern and understand that you [the whole church at Corinth] are God's temple (His sanctuary), and that God's Spirit has His permanent dwelling in you [to be at home in you, collectively as a church and also individually]?

I like this version because it underlines clearly what Paul was saying, "You are not just the temple of God collectively, but individually; each of you is a temple of God, and He lives (resides) in you!" This is not some random statement, preached in the heat of the moment, for Paul repeats it in First Corinthians 6. It is his revelation of who they really were, but it needed to become *their* revelation of who they really were for their lives to truly change.

> Or do you not know that your body is the temple of the Holy Spirit who is in you, whom you have from God, and you are not your own? (1 Corinthians 6:19)

Paul knew that his mission was to get them to see who and what they really were; when they did, that revelation would bring them to a new level of life and living. When it comes to our lives and leadership, we too must understand that we are no longer mere men and women, but God-filled temples. Great, ungodly leaders walk this, earth; they are just mere men with man's wisdom available to them. We are not; we are temples of God who hold the life, power, and wisdom of God and release it wherever we go.

Imagine with me a diagram of a body, neck, and head, and draw a dotted line through the neck. Unsaved leaders merely have neck-up ability (their own wisdom and understanding). We, as spiritual leaders, have neck-up ability and neck-down potential (God's Spirit in us leading and guiding us) which makes us so much more than mere leaders. It is vital right now that you see yourself as more than just "mere"! We were all just "mere" before we met Jesus, but when we believed in Him, we were delivered from being a "mere" anything to being God-filled temples carrying and sharing in His divine potential and nature.

> *...by which have been given to us exceedingly great and precious promises, that through these you may be partakers of the divine nature, having escaped the corruption that is in the world through lust* (2 Peter 1:4).

In the Old Testament, we read how God dwelt in and spoke out of the temples made by men, built according to His instructions. Today, we know that our New Covenant experience of God is that He no longer lives in temples of brick and fabric made by man, but in the very lives of the people He has redeemed. That's you and me and all who have come to Him by faith in the perfect, finished work of His only Son, Jesus. Just as God dwelt in and spoke out of those man-made temples of old, so today, He resides within and desires to speak from the temple-life of the believer. Spiritual leaders can know God's voice guiding and leading from deep within the now cleansed and holy temple courts of their lives.

Many thousands of books have been written on the subject of what it is to be spiritual. I am not trying to answer every question, and I am certainly not trying to cover every facet of the subject; my purpose for writing this chapter is to specifically look at how being spiritual empowers the leadership calling on our lives. So, forgive me if this does not answer every question you may have; I am, by design, trying to focus this discussion specifically toward the topic of spiritual leadership in our generation.

Being spiritual, to me, is simply a new birthright. It's about being open and able to hear the voice of God; it's about being led by Him in our everyday lives; it's about being a leader who does not just lead with worldly wisdom when needed but who can also release the wisdom and power of God into a situation when that's needed. It is truly about being a leader who has neck-up potential that can bless and neck-down potential that can make a difference—not "either/or" but "both/and"!

Let's face it; there are times you will need both. At times, with my five kids, I need to lead them with wise decisions, good principles, and leadership; at other times. I need to lay hands on them and believe for a healing or a touch of God for their lives. The spiritual leader is able to do both equally well; he or she has a healthy pendulum within that is well oiled and can swing where it is needed, when it is needed.

Not long ago, I was talking to a friend of mine who heads up a very well-known movement of churches in the UK and around the world; he told me of a personal situation that had happened in his home a few years previous. One day, after returning from a meeting, one of his daughters suddenly collapsed on the floor and was very ill. They called the doctors and were told that his daughter had the very serious strain of meningitis. In fact, they were told that she had just hours left to live and to prepare themselves to lose her. Being a father, my jaw dropped, and I made a statement that could have sounded flippant but was actually very sincere—and, later, we both felt, quite profound. It was a statement that started me thinking about a lot of what I am sharing with you in this book today. I said to him, "Wow, I suppose at that moment a leadership book by (I mentioned a famous renowned leadership author) could not help you. You needed Jesus Christ!"

Think about the truth of that statement for a moment. There are times in life when you need to draw upon the leadership principles you have learned, but there are other times when you need the power of God, and nothing else will do. You need to know how to touch and release Heaven! The good news is that my friend began praying for his daughter; he drew on the spiritual side of his spiritual leadership that day and saw her raised back to health. She is well and healthy to this day. Now, I am not knocking leadership books or their authors; I am simply noting that, sometimes in life, they cannot give you what you need. You need to know how to flow in the power of God that is yours through your union with Christ.

JESUS, THE SPIRITUAL LEADER

I am sure you will agree with me that Jesus will always be the greatest leader in history. There will never be a leader who equals Him. Jesus perfectly modeled spiritual leadership for us throughout the Gospels, and showed us by example what it looks like and what incredible things it can achieve. He regularly demonstrated both aspects of spiritual leadership and daily led so well. Look at how He raised up and released His team of disciples; how He taught people the principles of how to live well and make a difference through the Beatitudes of the Sermon on the Mount. These were and remain a pure work of art for those wanting leadership thinking and life-enhancing principles. But, as we all well know, He also released the power of Heaven into people's lives and situations. He was awesome at both, and lives were changed by both the leadership and the power of Heaven He dispensed daily.

Let's face it; many times He encountered people who needed His power, not only His incredible wisdom. His friend Lazarus did not need a seven-point message on walking with influence when he was dead; at that point, he needed the power of God to revive his very lifeless body. The woman with the issue of blood did not need a course on budgeting and managing her finances; she needed the power of God to stop the flow of blood that was killing her (though a budgeting course could have helped her later as we know she had spent all her money on doctors and was broke!).

Jesus was, in every way, a spiritual leader, and He calls each of us to be the same. I don't want to send the broken away with good advice; I want to see them liberated. I am tired of seeing people in healing lines get nice excuses and well-thought-out reasoning; I want to see them healed—how about you? I want to see more of the power of God, which heals and saves flowing through this life that loves Him, don't you?

JESUS MADE SPIRITUAL LOOK GOOD

Jesus walked around His generation as a spiritual leader, and He made spiritual look good; He made it attractive and desired, not repulsive and weird. Jesus modeled being spiritual in His generation in a way that was relevant and attractive—people never ran to get away from Him; rather, they daily lined up to get near Him. As we walk around our generation as twenty-first century spiritual leaders, we should not cause people to run for the hills; we should, like Jesus, have a divine draw and magnetism to our lives. People should want to be with us, near us, not in hiding from us. Let's make Jesus our blueprint for what a great leader is. He lived a very spiritual life that caused Him to have very natural crowd-control problems; He had multitudes of normal, everyday people who would not go home in between His meetings; He had to develop feeding programs for multitudes which sometimes involved taking little boys' picnics and supernaturally multiplying them. He made spirituality attractive and desired, not repulsive and freaky.

As He stood in that generation, being the spiritual leader that He had been called to be, people rushed to Him; they could not keep away from Him or get enough of Him. If you are being spiritual and everyone is running to get away from you, maybe you're just being weird. Maybe you need to look in the mirror and have an honest chat with yourself. Are you being a spiritual leader, or are you being a weirdo?

Recently, I have worked with a number of pastors and have helped them and their churches cross over into what God has for them now without having to rewind in any way to the things of yester year. We are hungry for the power of God flowing in our lives and in Church again, but no one wants to go back to the '50s or the '70s: that was then, and this is now. We are not welcoming back the weird and wonderful from years gone by or highlights from former moves of God;

we are saying, "God, we want the power of the Spirit as it looks—and needs to be—now, for our generation." When I told my church that we are going after the power of God, I added, "But our pursuit for the power of God does not mean we are going after the spooky or weird; in fact, it's good for you to know that Mrs. Weird and her weird cart are still banned." We don't want weird; we want God.

So let those who hunger after the past moments of glory keep their flags in their holsters, their gold dust in their pouches, and their other manifestations safely locked away. We don't want to model anything that was done in previous generations. We want the power of God and the moving of His Spirit as it needs to look and be for our generation. The only previous blueprint we want to build by is the one we find in the Book of Acts. We want that same Spirit to flow powerfully through us, making a difference now in our generation.

When it truly is God, as it was with Jesus, people will be drawn to it; they won't run from it. Think about it. Jesus was a walking, talking "move of the Spirit" because the Spirit was in Him; He lived a day-to-day life, empowered by the Holy Ghost. Notice that kids did not run away, crying and screaming things like, "Tell the weird man to go away." Notice that normal, everyday people did not lift an eyebrow and sarcastically say, "What's He on?" They were drawn to Him; they wanted to be around Him. My friends, when we let that same Holy Spirit have free access to the entirety of our lives, when we arise in our worlds, knowing we are not mere men but God's temples, we too will be "moves of the Spirit" in our communities; we too will see people drawn to us, not kicking down doors to get away from us; we too will be that light, that salt, that city on a hill.

JESUS' MASTER PLAN—TO UNLEASH SPIRITUAL LEADERS ON THE WORLD

We have spoken about Jesus the spiritual leader; now let us look at His disciples, the first team He personally raised up. In this section, we will also look at the master plan that Jesus had for sending that team into the world to make a difference.

As we read the final chapters of the Gospel of John, we see Jesus living out what He had prophesied would happen: He is betrayed, crucified, and buried; He then rises from the dead by the power of the Spirit. Then, in the final chapter of John and in the first chapter of Acts, He meets up with His team just prior to His ascension. This was a vital part of His master plan to change the earth.

The disciples meet their Lord again, now risen from the dead, in full health and strength—the same Jesus they had watched not long before die on a cross and be buried in a tomb. Now they are standing with their Lord and King, and He is alive and full of resurrection life. This must have fired them up big-time. Peter, now restored to his call, must have been getting the troops ready to march on the earth; even doubting Thomas, as he is known, was saying, "Yeah, let's do it!" There was a buzz in the camp; they were good to go, or so they thought, but something had to happen first. Let's look closely at what Jesus told them:

> The former account I made, O Theophilus, of all that Jesus began both to do and teach, until the day in which He was taken up, after He through the Holy Spirit had given commandments to the apostles whom He had chosen, to whom He also presented Himself alive after His suffering by many infallible proofs, being seen by them during forty days and speaking of the things pertaining to the kingdom of God. And being assembled together with them, He commanded them not to depart from Jerusalem, but to wait for the Promise of the Father, "which," He said, "you have heard from Me; for John truly baptized with water, but you shall be baptized with the Holy Spirit not many days from now." Therefore, when they had come together, they asked Him, saying, "Lord, will You at this time restore the kingdom to Israel?" And He said to them, "It is not for you to know times or seasons which

the Father has put in His own authority. But you shall receive power when the Holy Spirit has come upon you; and you shall be witnesses to Me in Jerusalem, and in all Judea and Samaria, and to the end of the earth" (Acts 1:1-8).

Notice the phrase in verse 4, "He commanded them not to depart." That's very strong language to use: Jesus "commanded them." Clearly, He was serious about this—but why? Why did He command them not to depart when His master plan was global evangelism? He had already given them the great commission: "Go into all the world." Why was He now telling them to wait? Did He want them to stay or go?

The answer is simple. He wanted them to go, but He loved them too much to send them as they presently were. Something powerful had to happen to each of them first: they needed an "upper room experience" to complete and equip them for the great commission. That upper room experience would turn them from leaders into spiritual leaders.

You see, they were indeed leaders. They had followed Him for three years, day and night, learning how to lead in a productive and effective way; they had sat daily under His teaching and mentorship. The problem was that they were not yet spiritual leaders; they had not yet received the baptism of the Holy Ghost; the resurrection life of Jesus had not yet possessed their mortal bodies and overshadowed their abilities. He knew that if they went now they might last a month, a year maybe, but they would not finish the courses He had for them to run.

We must remember that the same remains true for us. The ministry and His callings are not merely natural things, rather they are spiritual; and if we try to fulfill them using just our natural skills and abilities, we will never be able to. We will burn out or blow up. How can you juggle something divine and supernatural (which is what real ministry is) with mere carnal hands, attitudes, and abilities? Just as we are not only leaders, but spiritual leaders, we must remember that the Church also is not just an organization, it is a spiritual organization.

Jesus made an appointment for the disciples in an upper room, a divine appointment with the dimension of the Spirit that would turn them into the spiritual leaders they were called to be. God's plan still involved global evangelism, as we see in Acts 1:7. He says to them, "You shall be witnesses for Me locally, nationally, and to the ends of the earth"—which history records they indeed were.

Think about it: if those first-generation disciples who walked with Jesus needed the spiritual empowerment of the Holy Ghost to fulfill the leadership call and commission on their lives, how could we be so arrogant as to think that we don't?

NEXT STOP, THE UPPER ROOM

Our next stop in this unfolding story is the upper room in Jerusalem where we see the disciples waiting, not fully knowing what they were waiting for. What would it look like and feel like? We now own the Bible; it's easy for us. We have read what happened, but they were still writing it as they daily continued to walk by faith and obedience. They knew what Joel and Ezekiel had prophesied about this moment; they knew it had been described by Jesus as a gift from the Father; they knew He had said clearly to them, "No one is to go anywhere till after it has happened." They knew that His death was the true Passover for all humanity and that there must now be a Pentecost that would also affect humanity in a profound way. But they probably didn't really understand that what they were waiting for was not a something but a Someone—the Holy Spirit, sent from Heaven to empower, equip, comfort, and guide.

So they waited expectantly, praying, worshiping…and then suddenly:

…there came a sound from heaven, as of a rushing mighty wind, and it filled the whole house where they were sitting. Then there appeared to them divided tongues, as of fire, and one sat upon each of them. And they were all filled with the Holy

Spirit and began to speak with other tongues, as the Spirit gave them utterance (Acts 2:2-4).

The power of God, the very life of God, arrived in the room and then filled every one of them to overflowing. The Spirit of God filled the house and then broke off into individual tongues of fire that sat upon each one of them. This is important. God wanted to give them both a corporate and an individual experience with His Spirit. Why? Because He knew that they would be separated not long afterward; there would be many times when each disciple would be alone somewhere, without a corporate crowd experience to draw upon.

In those times, they would be as powerful individually as they were when they were gathered together. Each of them now stood complete as a spiritual leader, and now their leadership and lives were being enhanced and empowered from above. The Holy Spirit had come to live in them and had implanted within each of them His river that would indeed never run dry. Each of them, as Jesus had prophesied, had a river of life now flowing out of their innermost being, a miracle-making river that would shake the nations.

Each of their lives would later tell a story of the difference God's Spirit made that day in the upper room. Let's take a look at the life of Peter as one case study of radical change.

At the close of the Gospels, we see Peter deny Jesus in front of just three people, although he had contended adamantly that he would stand with Jesus to the end. The sad reality was that there, at the trial of Jesus, he denied his Lord three times. In his own strength and ability, with everything he had learned, before this tiny audience, he still denied Jesus. Then we turn a few pages into the Book of Acts and are introduced again to this man called Peter. He looks the same, speaks the same, yet he is not acting the same.

This is now post-upper room. The Spirit of God has been poured out; the resurrection life of Jesus is now resident within the lives of the disciples. Look at this man Peter now. Just after the upper room experience that is recorded in Acts 2, we see him preaching Jesus with passion, courage, and persuasion, communicating to a multitude about the saving grace of Jesus, the man he had once denied. Acts 2:41 tells us that 3,000 souls responded and were added to the church that day. Not bad for a man who, a short time before, could not stand up for Jesus in front of three people!

This, my friends, is the degree of change that happens when leaders get turned on spiritually. They move from a minus three ability to a plus three thousand potential because they are no longer living with a neck-up (self originated) potential alone; now they have the power of God residing within. Think about that for a moment. Peter's effect on the world went from minus three to plus three thousand when he crossed over from being a mere leader to being a spiritual leader.

I believe this is still the master plan and blueprint of Jesus today—to send out spiritual leaders to every part of the earth. When you look through the Book of Acts, you can actually see many times when both spirituality and good leadership operated in harmony together to produce a stable, dynamic, and effective church. To get three thousand people saved, as Peter did in Acts 2, was a spiritual thing; to manage them, to get them baptized, fed, and cared for took a whole lot of good leadership and effective management. They never had "either/or"; they had "both/and."

PAUL PUT THE SPIRITUAL FIRST

We have looked at Jesus as a spiritual leader and at His original, first-off-the-production-line disciples too. Now let's look at the apostle Paul. I don't know about you, but the apostle Paul is one of my heroes. His teaching was pure, undefiled revelation. His courage and his character were exemplary. He was one awesome guy. It's good for us to see where this incredible communicator and spiritual leader for his generation placed his confidence.

And I, brethren, when I came to you, did not come with excellence of speech or of wisdom declaring to you the testimony of God. For I determined not to know anything among you except Jesus Christ and Him crucified. I was with you in weakness, in fear, and in much trembling. And my speech and my preaching were not with persuasive words of human wisdom, but in demonstration of the Spirit and of power, that your faith should not be in the wisdom of men but in the power of God (1 Corinthians 2:1-5).

I personally believe that Paul was actually a great communicator and orator, yet he did not place his confidence in his eloquence or in his ability to speak. Neither did he place his confidence in the persuasive words of human wisdom, but rather in the power of His God, on the spiritual side of who he was. He placed his confidence in the demonstration of Spirit and power. When every modern concept and principle has been taught, people still need the power of God, manifest in the message we speak and tangibly released through our lives, to truly change.

When I look back over my salvation experience and the years that have followed, it becomes so evident to me that the most radical changes in my life were not the result of an eloquent message I heard or a well-constructed presentation, but of the power of God touching my life in remarkable ways. There might not have been thunder or lightning that moment I gave my life to Him, but His power certainly came and delivered me from my backslidden state; He turned my life around from failure and ruin to success and destiny. His power got me back on my feet when I fell over; His power also got me running strong again when I ran out of steam.

Yes, I do thank God for the leadership wisdom that many have sown, and still sow into my life, which gives great guidance and understanding, but I could never exchange what I have known and tasted of the power of God for the wisdom of man. Paul closes this profound statement in First Corinthians 2 by placing emphasis on the power and the Spirit because he wants people to attach their faith to those things rather than to persuasive words: "That your faith should not be in the wisdom of men but in the power of God" (1 Cor. 2:5). Paul knew that people needed the spiritual realities of Christianity in order to make it.

In the earlier days of my walk with God, godly leaders gave me many "spiritual tools" to be used as the everyday instruments of an effective believer: praying in the Holy Ghost, prophesy, prayer, and all the other power tools and gifts of the Spirit. Knowing about them as a young believer helped me to break through to the victories that I have known throughout my walk with God. My point is simple. If we needed spiritual tools to make it this far, you better believe that the young Christians we are raising up will need them too. How can we expect them to get where we did, and indeed beyond, if we do not allow them to know about the spiritual tools that were handed to us and that we used?

As New Covenant churches we have a responsibility before God to raise up the next generation of believers, not just to understand great leadership, but also to desire and handle spiritual things. Our challenge is to teach them about spirituality and spiritual gifts in a way that is relevant to the twenty-first century without losing any of the dynamics or power. If we legislate manifestations of the power of God or the flowing of His Spirit in the Church because of a desire to be seeker-friendly, we will not shine like we were destined and designed to. The Church must be known for good leadership, but she must also be known for the power and the presence of God. Let us always remember that first we are called to be spiritual, because that is what we are. When His Spirit came to live in us, at that moment, we became spiritual (Spirit-filled) people; to be a *leader* is a natural outworking of being *spiritual*.

Recently, I heard people debating about the whole issue of safety and the supernatural; ideas were exchanged about what we should allow and what we should not with regard to supernatural or unusual things happening in church. A couple of days later, I was considering that discussion, and I felt God's Spirit say to me, "Whose house is it anyway?" When I thought about this, I thought of my own home and how no one has the right to tell me what I can do in it because it's mine. In the same way, in all of our discussions on making church safe, we need to make sure that we are not stopping God's Spirit from doing what He wants to do in His own house.

WHAT A SPIRITUAL LEADER HAS

There are a number of things that a spiritual leader has that a natural leader does not. I want to look at a few of them here and get you excited about the potential you have as a spiritual leader.

1. God's Spirit Speaking Daily Within the Temple of Your Life

What an awesome thought! The same Spirit that raised Christ from the dead now lives within the hearts of spiritual leaders and daily speaks the thoughts and intentions of the Father. Wow! I have more going for me than some of the top CEOs of international companies. They may have great above-the-neck potential, but I have the Spirit of God speaking to and leading me from deep within.

Look at this passage from the Amplified Bible; it brings this fact out so colorfully:

> *I have still many things to say to you, but you are not able to bear them or to take them upon you or to grasp them now. But when He, the Spirit of Truth (the Truth-giving Spirit) comes, He will guide you into all the Truth (the whole, full Truth). For He will not speak His own message [on His own authority]; but He will tell whatever He hears [from the Father; He will give the message that has been given to Him], and He will announce and declare to you the things that are to come [that will happen in the future]. He will honor and glorify Me, because He will take of (receive, draw upon) what is Mine and will*

reveal (declare, disclose, transmit) it to you. Everything that the Father has is Mine. That is what I meant when I said that He [the Spirit] will take the things that are Mine and will reveal (declare, disclose, transmit) it to you (John 16:12-15 AMP).

I love how the Amplified puts that. Jesus is teaching, preparing His leadership team for when He is gone; He introduces them to the third Person of the Godhead—the Holy Spirit—and reveals that He is coming not just to give them goose bumps in meetings, but to daily lead and guide them, to reveal things to them. My friends, it is the same for us. The Holy Spirit has not been withdrawn from the world but still lives in the heart of every born-again believer who has received Him. Read the words from John 16 nice and slow; let them sink in: "When He comes, He will guide you into all truth; He will tell you what He hears the Father say. He will announce, declare, and transmit to you the things that are God's."

Listen, when believers say they don't hear God, I believe it is primarily a sign that they need to develop their ability to listen, to train their ears to recognize His voice. The Spirit of God lives within you and transmits and reveals what you should do next; we need to be ever developing our spiritual ears to hear.

2. The Mind of Christ—The Known Wisdom of God for Any Situation

We do, however, speak a message of wisdom among the mature, but not the wisdom of this age or of the rulers of this age, who are coming to nothing. No, we declare God's wisdom, a mystery that has been hidden and that God destined for our glory before time began. None of the rulers of this age understood it, for if they had, they would not have crucified the Lord of glory. However, as it is written: "What no eye has seen, what no ear has heard, and what no mind has conceived"—the things God has prepared for those who love Him—these are the things God has revealed to us by His Spirit (1 Corinthians 2:6-10 NIV).

These verses tell us that there is a wisdom available that is far above the wisdom of this world; if we walk as spiritual leaders, this wisdom is made available to us for our everyday lives by the Spirit of God who resides within us. When we speak, we will speak with a wisdom that is from God that has been hidden from unsaved man from before time began.

Carry on reading what Paul says—it gets better:

> *The Spirit searches all things, even the deep things of God. For who knows a person's thoughts except their own spirit within them? In the same way no one knows the thoughts of God except the Spirit of God. What we have received is not the spirit of the world, but the Spirit who is from God, so that we may understand what God has freely given us. This is what we speak, not in words taught us by human wisdom but in words taught by the Spirit, explaining spiritual realities with Spirit-taught words. The person without the Spirit does not accept the things that come from the Spirit of God but considers them foolishness, and cannot understand them because they are discerned only through the Spirit. The person with the Spirit makes judgments about all things, but such a person is not subject to merely human judgments, for, "Who has known the mind of the Lord so as to instruct Him?" But we have the mind of Christ* (1 Corinthians 2:10-16).

Paul makes some incredible statements concerning what is available to Spirit-filled believers and leaders. Each of them is worth further study and thought:

- The Spirit knows the thoughts of God and reveals them to us.

- We have received the Spirit of God, not the spirit of this world.

- We do not speak just man's wisdom, but God's.

- The spiritual person can make great judgments about all things.

Paul leaves the best statement till last: "We have the mind of Christ." That's worth thinking about.

These verses run directly alongside what we read in John when Jesus taught His disciples about the Holy Spirit (see John 14:15-18,25-26; 16:5-15). Such passages assure us that God has placed His Spirit within us; He longs to daily guide and lead us with a wisdom that natural leaders simply do not have. The Holy Spirit provides a clear communication line between you and God, and He can now communicate directly to the spiritual part of who you are. It's like a divine umbilical cord: "But he who is joined to the Lord is one spirit with Him" (1 Cor. 6:17).

Here's a good way of looking at it: when you were born naturally (your first birth), you came into the world connected to your mother by an umbilical cord; through that cord she gave you everything you needed to live. Then the doctor came along and cut the cord, and you were on your own. When you are born again (your second birth), you are born again spiritually; according to First Corinthians, you are one spirit with the Lord. The good news is that that cord is not cut and the believer remains connected to the Lord by the Spirit of God who is both in Heaven and with us. Learn to draw on the life and leading of God's Spirit who is now in you.

It is vital that we understand what has been made available to us as spiritual people and leaders; we don't live our lives by the mere wisdom of this age, but by the wisdom we find in God. Spiritual leaders have higher wisdom constantly available to them.

3. Dynamite in Their Guts

Jesus said to His first generation of leadership, "You shall receive power when the Holy Ghost comes upon you." Jesus was not sending His spiritual leaders out weak or dependent on their own resources; He placed the *dunamis* (dynamite power) of Heaven within each of them. They had the supernatural power of God available for whatever situation they faced. Here's more good news for you: if you're a believer, you are meant to walk in spiritual leadership—in whatever sphere the Lord has placed you. You too have this supernatural power available to you. The same power of the Holy Spirit is in your life. We all need to draw on and depend on Him so much more than we currently do.

A SPIRITUAL RIVER WILL FLOW FROM YOU

On the last day, that great day of the feast, Jesus stood and cried out, saying, "If anyone thirsts, let him come to Me and drink. He who believes in Me, as the Scripture has said, out of his heart will flow rivers of living water." But this He spoke concerning the Spirit, whom those believing in Him would receive; for the Holy Spirit was not yet given, because Jesus was not yet glorified (John 7:37-39).

Jesus boldly stood up on the last day of this great feast and prophesied what was to come for all those who would believe in Him. He said that out of their hearts—other translations say "bellies" (I, being from Portsmouth, use the word "guts"), rivers of living water would flow. I love that He did not promise puddles, babbling brooks, calm lakes, or gentle streams; He promised *rivers*. Over the years, many theologians have tried to reason out what He was saying in these verses. If you read on, it becomes quite clear: "This He spoke concerning the Spirit." Jesus was speaking of the Spirit of God who was with Him and who would come upon the lives of all believers.

As you read the words of Jesus, you see that there was a systematic process He went through that has now been fulfilled. Jesus said the Spirit had not yet been given because Jesus was not yet glorified. Anyone ready for some more good news? The Bible reveals that Jesus has been glorified, the Spirit has been given, and He is available today for all who place their faith in Jesus. The only thing stopping the flow of the river of life is the believer himself—if he refuses to acknowledge and receive what God has made so freely available. It's that river, flowing from the heart of who you are, that positions you in life as a spiritual leader who is called, appointed, and anointed.

WHAT DOES DAY-TO-DAY SPIRITUAL LEADERSHIP LOOK LIKE?

As I have said so many times already, spiritual leadership should never look freaky or weird; it is simply everyday, normal people doing super-normal things in Jesus' name. To me, a great picture of this can be found in Acts 3:

> *Now Peter and John went up together to the temple at the hour of prayer, the ninth hour. And a certain man lame from his mother's womb was carried, whom they laid daily at the gate of the temple which is called Beautiful, to ask alms from those who entered the temple; who, seeing Peter and John about to go into the temple, asked for alms. And fixing his eyes on him, with John, Peter said, "Look at us." So he gave them his attention, expecting to receive something from them. Then Peter said, "Silver and gold I do not have, but what I do have I give you: In the name of Jesus Christ of Nazareth, rise up and walk." And he took him by the right hand and lifted him up, and immediately his feet and ankle bones received strength. So he, leaping up, stood and walked and entered the temple with them—walking, leaping, and praising God* (Acts 3:1-8).

I love this account of an incredible miracle taking place on the streets of this city because it is such a normal, everyday picture. Peter and John are on their way to a prayer meeting; they are probably chatting away about anything and everything, and then, suddenly, they come upon a man with a need. This man was begging because he had no other options in life. First, what made Peter and John spiritual leaders was that they did not ignore the man and his need; spiritual leaders don't ignore people in times of need—they don't "cross the road." Then, they turned to the man and, with confidence, let him know that, while they had no cash, they had something much better. Where did that confidence come from? They knew they had a river of life within them, waiting for the opportunity to flow out. "Sir," Peter said, "we have no money, but here is something you need more. In the name of Jesus, get up and walk." He then reached down, without even asking whether the man wanted to or not, and lifted him to his feet. The power of God was released, the man's legs were healed, and he started jumping around. Miracle delivered; man's life changed! What an awesome account! What blesses me is that it does not say:

- They were praying on the way to the prayer meeting.

- They got a choir and started singing "hallelujah" a multitude of times in various keys, till they "felt it."

- They called the rest of the team and prayed about it for ten hours.

- They went away and prayed in the Holy Ghost for an hour in a corner "binding and loosing" everything in sight, leaving the man to wonder what was going on.

Instead, they reached out and released the resurrection power of Jesus into the life of this man who needed some help getting back onto his feet. In this case, the man did not need great principles and concepts; he needed the power of God. A leadership series would have been no good to him; maybe he could have used one later as he re-built his life, but, at this moment, he needed what only a spiritual leader could give. What a crazy picture it would have been if John had handed him a workbook on seven ways to effectively beg or if Peter had given him a CD set on effectively managing finances! No, they gave him what Jesus had for him. Spiritual leaders are God's postmen, delivering heavenly things to earthly people.

I don't know about you, but as I walk around life, I often "happen upon" people who need help getting back on their feet. Sometimes they are crippled by relational problems; other times their problems are financial or physical, but they're crippled and need help. The spiritual leader can bend down and help them, sometimes with wisdom and at other times with power. I want to be able to give them whatever they need to get back on their feet; how about you?

SPIRITUALLY NATURAL AND NATURALLY SPIRITUAL

It's OK to be normal. You don't have to be weird to be spiritual; God wants to empower you, just as you are. When you know He is in you, great things begin to happen, and the glory goes to God. If Jesus was walking the earth today, He would not be wearing a long, seamless gown; He would probably be wearing a good pair of jeans and a T-shirt. He would be wearing what the people of the culture He had come to reach were wearing. People would run to Him today just as they ran to Him then. Why? Because Jesus is not weird or spooky; He is wonderfully relevant. So, let's make sure we are not being weird or spooky either as we seek to be the best spiritual leaders we can be. Like the disciples in Acts 3, let's walk through life living for God, ready to make a difference in someone's world when we come across them—I call it "miracles in blue jeans."

INVEST IN BOTH COMPONENTS

So finally, if we want to be effective spiritual leaders, we need to be ready to invest in both parts of the title. We need to be investing in the spiritual side of who we are on a regular basis. We also need to be investing in our leadership side. As I mentioned earlier, the pendulum of your life needs to be able to touch both parts of the call, and you need to live daily embracing and developing both.

Hopefully, this chapter has called different people to different decisions. For some of you, that may involve praying a little less and getting your hands on some leadership training tools, doing something to increase your leadership capacity and ability. For others, that may mean that it is time to rediscover the spiritual side of your leadership potential; it's time to let God open the cupboard under the stairs in your life and turn the power back on.

To be honest, that was me. I ran after leadership development with a passion, which was not wrong and was much needed, believe me. Yet one day, a while ago, I felt God tapping my shoulder and telling me to go back and pick up some of the spiritual things I had dropped along the way. For me, these were the simple things I used to do—like speaking in tongues, having strong devotions, and so on. As I have been rediscovering these powerful things in my life, I have also found that I do not have to lose any elements of good leadership; they live so well together in the life of the spiritual leader.

Some of you need to go out and invest in the leadership side of your call; others need to rediscover or find for the first time your spiritual dynamic. I encourage you to go for it; invest in your life. Don't settle for being just a leader—be the spiritual leader God has called you to be. Remember, it's not "either/or" but "both/and"!

Our nations, our cities, and our families need us to arise and be the spiritual men and women—and the spiritual leaders— God has called us to be!

ENDNOTE

1. "Synergy"; see http://www.thefreedictionary.com/synergy.

DO YOU KNOW JESUS?

I hope you enjoyed this book and that is has been both a blessing and a challenge to your life and walk with God. Maybe you just got hold of it and are looking through it before starting. Long ago, I made the decision never to take for granted that everyone has prayed a prayer to receive Jesus as their Lord, so I am including this prayer as my finale. If you have never asked Jesus into your life and would like to do that now, it's so easy. Just pray this simple prayer:

Dear Lord Jesus, thank You for dying on the cross for me. I believe that You gave Your life so that I could have life. When You died on the cross, You died as an innocent man who had done nothing wrong. You were paying for my sins and the debt I could never pay. I believe in You, Jesus, and receive the brand-new life and fresh start that the Bible promises that I can have. Thank You for my sins forgiven, for the righteousness that comes to me as a gift from You, for hope and love beyond what I have known, and the assurance of eternal life that is now mine. Amen.

Here are a few good next moves: Get yourself a Bible that is easy to understand and begin to read. Maybe start in the Book of John so you can discover all about Jesus for yourself. Start to pray—prayer is simply talking to God—and, finally, find a church that's alive and get your life planted in it. These simple ingredients will cause your relationship with God to grow.

Why not email me and let me know if you took this step so I can rejoice with you?

Response@greatbiglife.co.uk

ABOUT THE AUTHOR

Andy and Gina Elmes are the senior pastors of Family Church, a multi-congregational church located on the south coast of England. Andy is a visionary leader who has grown the church from twelve people on its first day to a significant and influential church in the UK and beyond.

Andy is also the founder of Synergy Network, a fellowship of like-minded ministers who desire inspirational relationships and growth in their leadership, ministries, and lives, independent of what type or style of church they lead. He is also the founder of "Great Big Life," a ministry established to see people equipped and empowered not only to lead effectively in church but also in every other sphere of life.

Andy has a wealth of experience and wisdom to offer that comes from a very successful time in ministry. As well as planting churches, he has been involved in many forms of evangelism including travelling as an evangelist for many years across the UK and throughout the world. A dynamic visionary, Andy helps people to see things outside of the box; as a strategist, he helps others to set goals within their lives and ministries and move toward them quickly. His experience, combined with his life-coaching skills, makes him a valuable asset to any pastor or leader seeking personal development and encouragement.

A highly sought-after conference speaker for events and conferences, Andy regularly shares on a whole range of subjects including leadership, motivation, and evangelism.

Andy's versatility allows him to communicate as a pastor, an evangelist, a teacher, and a coach reaching individuals of all ages and in a variety of settings. Andy is very natural and irreligious in his approach, using humor well and being very animated and often unconventional in his delivery. His desire is to lead people to Jesus and help them to discover all that is now available to them through what Jesus has done for them. His personal mandate is "to know the King and to advance His Kingdom."

Andy and Gina, along with their five children, Olivia, Ethan, Gabrielle, Sophie, and Christina, reside in Portsmouth, England.

CONTACT THE AUTHOR

For more information about Andy Elmes and the ministries he oversees, or to order more copies of this book, use the following contact information:

Address: PO Box 240
Southsea, Hants, PO2 7YE, UK

Telephone: 44 23 9266 2257
Email: info@greatbiglife.co.uk

Additional Ministry Web Sites:

Great Big Life ministry site:
www.greatbiglife.co.uk

Family Church site:
www.family-church.org.uk

Synergy network site:
www.synergy-network.co.uk

Synergy Christian Churches site:
www.synergychristianchurches.org

Additional copies of this book and other book
titles from EVANGELISTA MEDIA™
and DESTINY IMAGE™ EUROPE
are available at your local bookstore.

We are adding new titles every month!

To view our complete catalog online, visit us at:
www.evangelistamedia.com

Send a request for a catalog to:

Via della Scafa, 29/14
65013 Città Sant'Angelo (Pe), ITALY
Tel. +39 085 4716623 • Fax +39 085 9090113
info@evangelistamedia.com

"Changing the World, One Book at a Time."

Are you an author?

Do you have a "today" God-given message?

CONTACT US

We will be happy to review your manuscript
for the possibility of publication:

publisher@evangelistamedia.com
http://www.evangelistamedia.com/pages/AuthorsAppForm.htm